THE MIND

THE MIND OF THE FATHERS

by

George S. Bebis

HOLY CROSS ORTHODOX PRESS

Brookline, Massachusetts 02146

We, gratefully acknowledge that funds
for the publication of this book have
graciously been provided by the
ARCHBISHOP IAKOVOS LEADERSHIP
100 ENDOWMENT FUND

Published by Holy Cross Orthodox Press
50 Goddard Avenue
Brookline, Massachusetts 02146

Cover design by Michael Sitaras

Library of Congress Cataloging in Publication Data
Bebis, George S.
The mind of the fathers: essays in patristic studies
by George S. Bebis.
p. cm.
ISBN 0-916586-73-1
1. Fathers of the church, Greek. 2. Religious thought—To 600.
I. Title.
BR67.B375 1994   93-50532
230'.042—dc20   CIP

Table of Contents

For
BISHOP METHODIOS
President of Hellenic College-Holy Cross
Greek Orthodox School of Theology in recognition
of his many sacrifices on behalf of our Mother-School

Introduction

I am most grateful to His Grace Bishop Methodios of Boston, President of Hellenic College/Holy Cross Greek Orthodox School of Theology, who urged me to collect and publish some of my basic works which express and represent my thought and teaching on the theology, the life, and the praxis of the Fathers of the Church. Indeed these works in this first volume represent what I have articulated throughout my experience as both a student and a teacher of the Fathers. They have inspired my whole life and have blessed my whole existence. The mind and the spirit of the Fathers of the Church have guided and have led me to the pastures of their unfailing faith and their unceasing prayer to Christ our Lord and Savior.

It is not easy to enter and grasp the "phronema" of the Fathers, to feel and hear the agonies and the triumphs of their hearts. But in studying their works and comtemplating their lives, one can see, with the help of the Almighty, the impact Christ had upon them and the liberating power of the Holy Spirit upon every aspect of their thought and endeavor. They were both practical and contemplative men — holy men — who enjoyed both the "kataphatic way" as well as the "apophatic way" of approaching and reaching the divine life. This is why they appear, almost always, down to earth and ready to acknowledge the failures of human nature in the most vivid way. "The Church has become a wreckage," Saint Basil the Great writes with exasperation, and Saint Gregory the Theologian complains bitterly that "Christ is sleeping," while Saint Chrysostom laments that many of the clergy of his time are unworthy of their calling. In this context they realized the dangerous temptation of "akedia" or despondency, or spiritual "wearisomeness" of which no one was immune. Therefore they constantly advised "diakrisis," or discernment, and patience, and love for all. Mere asceticism without "diakrisis" is unacceptable for the Fathers. Love and philanthropy were their supreme goal and attainment and the strictness and seriousness of their purpose never diminished the spirit of forgiveness and understanding they showed even towards their adversaries. Saint Cyril demanded nothing else from Nestorios but that he accept the Orthodox doctrine on Theotokos and any personal animosity would have been forgotten. Saint Symeon the New Theologian, a stern monk himself with an

unyielding monastic commitment, is ready to forgive and forget as long
as his opponents are good practicing Christians. And Saint Gregory of
Nyssa, returning to his diocese with tears in his eyes, offers forgiveness
and love even to those who have been so unjust towards him.

But the "phronema" or the mind of the Fathers finds its most
beautiful expression in the healthy concept which they have for the Christian spiritual life. They envision the unending effort towards perfection
as a continuous climbing on the "klimax" or the "ladder of the divine
ascent," or a constant and invariable ascending towards the "brilliant
cloud," high up on the very peak of the spiritual Mount Sinai, where
the divine energies of God abide and reside and may be met and united
with the human nature, as Saint Gregory of Nyssa so dramatically writes.
And speaking about Mount Sinai, we must add here that the Fathers
never espoused extreme and unbecoming accomplishments to human
nature. Moderation was their priority and their advice to their spiritual
children. The "right" and the "left," the "conservative" and "liberal,"
understanding of life were alien to their balanced view of spiritual fulfilment. This attachment of the Fathers to "moderation" or "the middle
way" preserved in them the genuine spirit of humility and guarded them
from any excess of overzealous faithful. This blessed virtue of humility
kept them in the proper spiritual frame-work and helped them to con-
quer all the worldly enticements of gluttony, impurity, avarice, arrogance,
and infidelity. This is why they broke the wall of separation between the
divine and human, and this is why, also, they had developed the vision
of a sound understanding of history, where divine and human meet and
where the will and the glory of God become ultimate realities and
experiences.

It is not accidental that in the fifties, a Protestant writer, Robert
Payne, published two volumes, one on the Western Fathers of the Church
and another volume on Fathers of the Eastern Church. The title of the
second volume was *The Holy Fire*. Indeed, this holy fire consumed and
brightened and animated and "glowed" in the lives of the Fathers. This
holy fire exalted them and led them to complete purity and freedom from
evil and liberation from passions. Thus, they become "vessels" of
God and they were cleansed thoroughly, they were illumined blissful-
ly, and they were "divinized" and "perfected" so convincingly. They
have tested the heavenly joy of the Lord, they emerged and immersed
into the sweetness of the supernatural fruits of the Holy Spirit, they

became one with the "One," the "Beloved One," Jesus Christ our Savior. This is why their example has become indispensible for all the students of the holy Scriptures and for those who really want to become real participants with the treasures of our liturgical and spiritual life. We cannot comprehend the spirit of the holy Scripture, the history of the Church, the Orthodox Tradition, and the traditions of our Faith unless we study seriously and wholesomely the lives and the thought of the Fathers. I pray that this small volume, a small token of love to the Fathers, may become a true source of inspiration for our lives. This could happen, through the prayers of our holy Fathers, now and forever and ever. Amen.

Now it only remains for me to thank the Rev. Dr. N. Michael Vaporis for his unfailing support and assistance in the preparation of this volume for the press. His advice and comments will always be remembered. I would also add here my deepest gratitude to His Eminence Archbishop Iakovos who has always favored me with his encouragement and assistance throughout my tenure at Hellenic College/Holy Cross.

G. S. B.

The Concept of Tradition
in the Fathers of the Church

Tradition has always been one of the most fascinating and most controversial themes among the serious thinkers and scholars of the Church.

The basic question "What is Tradition?" has attracted both contemporary theologians and historians as well as great Fathers of the Church and numerous ecclesiastical writers of the early Christian age.

What is the essence and the scope of Tradition? Does Tradition really concern and refer only to the past? What are the origins of Tradition and what are its relations with the Scriptures and the early Christian "kerygma"? Is Tradition inspired by the Holy Spirit? Should Tradition be understood as something external, a body and a set of pronouncements which exist apart from the essence and the structure of the Church? Is it a historical "horizontal" evolution and evaluation of the Christian teaching? Is it a formation of various norms and molds, static or mobile, which have shaped the Christian life and teaching?

Many attempts have been made to define and explain Tradition, especially since the times of the Enlightenment. Tradition was thought to be a product of the human reason, a natural process of the development of human thought, a poignant and outwardly expressive endeavor to interpret the Christian past in terms of analytical philosophy and dialectical methodology. But sheer rationalism could not offer a solution for the understanding of Tradition. Neither Schleiermacher's principle of religious experience nor Ritschl's "communal moralism" contributed to the explanation of the inner meaning of Tradition. An unfortunate severing and organic rupture between Scripture and Tradition occurred when the disciples and the successors of the first German Reformers drew a sharp line of distinction between Scriptures and ecclesiastical tradition

1

and when Roman Catholic scholars reacted by subjecting Tradition to the doctrine of Papal infallibility. Harnack's attempt to explain the reality of Tradition as a plague of "Traditionalismus" which cut off the life of the Church from her pure primitive roots, and Barth's and Brunner's "anti-historical" stand and finally all sorts of form-criticism, demythologizing and "de-theologizing" the history of the Church, have put Tradition under the scrutiny of a new form of contemporary rationalism, without providing, however, the discovery of the proper perspective and scope under which Tradition should be studied and evaluated.

In order to achieve that perspective, it is of paramount importance to see how the Fathers of the Church approached the concept of Tradition. But why should we go back to the Fathers? Vincent of Lerins in his *Commentary* (434 A. D.) speaks about "the holy fathers . . . who, each in his own time and place, remaining in the unity of communion and the faith, were accepted as approved masters. . . ."[1] All enchiridia of patrology characterize the Fathers of the Church as combining holiness of life, orthodoxy of doctrine, ecclesiastical approval and antiquity.[2] No serious patrologist would argue today for antiquity as the necessary qualification for a Father of the Church, for many holy men lived after the eighth century (which is set as the chronological limit of the Patristic era).[3] Saint Photios, Saint Symeon the New Theologian, and Saint Gregory Palamas are ample examples of men who rightly are called Fathers in the Orthodox Church.[4]

Saint John of Damascus speaking about Saint John Chrysostom, clearly defines him as a man who studies and searches the Scriptures, explains and interprets them, bringing up the hidden truths and exposing the esoteric beauty of them; the Father succeeds in his work through and with the help of the prophetic Holy Spirit.[5] The Fathers of the Church are not an exclusive group of men, even holy men, who had kept for themselves the right to interpret the Scriptures and write and express the teaching of the Church, or men who merely tried to keep the rule of faith in accordance with the apostolic tradition. They are primarily men who live "in the depth of the Holy Spirit,"[6] who continuously ascend towards the "luminous darkness,"[7] and who finally enjoy not only the writings about the Holy Trinity but who live in communion with the Holy Trinity.[8]

Thus the Fathers could not be compared with contemporary scholars who are almost or completely alien and unfamiliar with the life in the incomprehensible vastness of the Holy Trinity. Form criticism, an ill-inspired *historicism*, or sheer rationalism are foreign to the Orthodox patristic tradition. This does not mean at all that contemporary means and modern scientific methods should be ignored in the study of the Scriptures and the Fathers. Even historical criticism is welcomed when practiced reverently. But to try to find an antithesis or an antinomy between the Fathers and contemporary *historicism* shows a deficient understanding of Orthodox ecclesiology and Orthodox pneumatology. To be sure, the Fathers of the Church were interested immensely in history. However, for them history is the great scene where the *Magnalis Dei* take place; for them historical continuity was of paramount importance for it was linked with the historical experience of the Church whose aim was and still is the salvation of mankind through Christ and in Christ. The Fathers of the Church were also men of knowledge, well-versed in almost all the sciences of their times; they were men of strong convictions, brilliant minds and great vision. Critical methodology was not foreign to them and they knew how to use all the means of intellectual argumentation. But above and beyond all these human charismata, the Fathers of the Church should not be studied apart of the communion— to use again the expression of Vincent of Lerins[9]—of the whole Church. Every student of theology knows the famous dictum: "unanimis consensus Patrum," as the unanimous consent of the Fathers and the agreement of the Fathers concerning "the true and catholic doctrine of the Church, without any doubt or scruple."[10] This common opinion among the Fathers should not be taken numerically but morally,[11] or to put it more correctly ecclesiologically. That means that they speak from within the Church and for the Church, and more importantly they do live and fully experience the life of the Church. Thus Canon 19 of the Synod of Trullo which admonishes the people of God not to go "beyond the limits now fixed, no varying from the tradition of the God-bearing fathers . . ."[12] should not be construed as an admonition which forbids the study and research of the holy Scriptures, nor it should be thought as contradictory to the statement of Gregory the Theologian who encourages "philosophizing" about the world, the soul and even about Christ.[13] Both Gregory the Theologian and the Canon 19 of Trullo (A. D. 692) aim at the same purpose, namely, the edification of the people of God in the spirit and in the living reality of the Church. Besides, one must not forget that the same Father emphatically states that "Not to everyone, my friends, does it belong to philosophize about God; not to everyone—the subject is not so cheap and low—and I will add, not before every audience, nor at all times, nor on all points; but on certain occasions, and before certain persons, and within certain limits."[14]

It has been correctly stated "that the great Fathers knew of no patristic key.''[15] We do also agree that the patristic scholar "cannot validly interpret the New Testament by patristic criteria alone.''[16] Nevertheless the Fathers of the Church should not be considered apart of the Church, or as isolated elite in the Church, not at all. The Fathers of the Church "breathe the Holy Spirit," to use the expression of Saint Anthony,[17] but at the same time all the people of God "breathe the Holy Spirit." The clergy, the monks and the laymen are members of the Church of God. Moreover, not only the life and writings of the Fathers depict the life of the Church. The local creeds, the ecumenical councils, as Christian architecture and iconography, and philanthropic works exercised in the Church are the testimonies which express the totality and the wholeness of the mystery of salvation. Thus the separation of the Fathers from the rest of the life of the Church is alien to Orthodox ecclesiology. We must also bear in mind that the patristic tradition did not stop at the Synod of Trullo. Great Fathers of the Church, as we pointed out already, have lived throughout the history of the Church and undoubtedly they are still living among us (minus antiquity). What of Saint Nikodemos the Hagiorite, or Saint Nektarios of Aigina, or even Chrysostomos Papadopoulos? Fr. Sergius Bulgakov rightly remarked that Tradition "is not an archaeological museum, not a scientific catalogue, it is not furthermore a dead depository.''[18] We shall add that the most specific patristic tradition is not merely a listing of the names of the Fathers, neither a numerical citing of their pronouncements, nor they do consist of a lifeless mechanical apparatus or device through which we can solve our problems by refining intellectual exercises. They should be considered as carriers of the Holy Spirit, as Christ-bearing guides for our spiritual ascent, as the bond between the Gospel and the apostolic teaching, as members who live in the fullness of the life of the Church. Therefore any attempt to break the bond between Scripture and patristic tradition should be construed as rupture and a "schism" in the historical process and experience of the Church. Also to claim that certain doctrines (as for instance original sin) are found in the Fathers but not in the Bible, is not only an arbitrary biblicalism; it shows at the same time that the fullness of the Church both in space and time is ignored and the energies of the Holy Spirit are restricted in certain specific chronological limits of a specific chronological era. To be sure, the Fathers of the Church were always anxious to sustain their teaching on biblical grounds, but they have been gifted with the intrinsic inspiration and intuition, with the divine light and perception to see and acknowledge the mysterious and secret teaching which were hidden behind the lines of the Scripture. In other words, the doctrine of the divine inspiration is equally important for both the authors of the Scriptures as well as for the Fathers.

Do all these mean that there is a deep difference and chasm between biblical studies and patristic tradition? Of course not, especially when we look at both as the accumulative experience of the Church united in Christ and led by the Holy Spirit to the fulfillment of the eschaton. One point, however, must be made clear, and that is that we cannot study the Scripture without the Fathers of the Church. *Sola Scriptura* or *Sola Traditio* have no place in the scheme of the Orthodox Theology. "Scripture and Fathers" are referred to and quoted together, because Scripture cannot be studied and interpreted without the Fathers. There is no doubt that the Fathers were the great exegetes and interpreters of Scripture and it is most significant that almost all the Fathers wrote and preached on the Bible. They were "the eyes of the Church,"[19] and used all the hermeneutical principles and methods so that they might convey the biblical message of salvation to their fellow men. Such being the case, it is right to say that "Scripture without interpretation is not Scripture at all; the moment it is used and becomes alive it is always interpreted Scripture."[20] Here, of course, we find not a *patristic key* to the Bible, but rather the testimony of the Church to the Scripture and the witness of the Holy Spirit in the Church. In other words, the Fathers exercising their hermeneutical and teaching task, acted as instruments of the Holy Trinity and as the perennial witness of the presence of the Holy Trinity in the Church.

Now it is not in the scope of this paper to discuss the relation of Scripture and Tradition as such. Professor Nikos Nissiotis does this adequately in his well-written article on *The Unity of Scripture and Tradition: An Eastern Orthodox Contribution to the Prolegomena of Hermeneutics.*[21] Professor Nissiotis established convincingly that there is no tension or opposition that exists between the written and oral tradition: that oral tradition precedes the written form of the Gospel and that in the early Church as well as later in the apostolic Church there was an absolute unity between the Bible and Tradition.[22] Nor shall we examine here the concept of Tradition in both the Old Testament and the New Testament, neither in the Jewish manner of the transmission of inherited truths, nor to philosophical and especially the Platonic concept of esoteric tradition.[23]

Etymologically speaking, the term tradition both in its Greek original word παράδοσις and its Latin equivalent *traditio* does not mean merely transmission or transference of certain things or ideas from one person to another. In both biblical and patristic context it means gift, giving, offering, delivering, and even performing benevolences and charity. But in the whole context of biblical and patristic theology, Tradition is more than that. It is the life of a person,[24] and more exactly the life of the whole Trinity as revealed by Christ and testified by the Holy Spirit. Tradition both in the Scripture begins from the Holy Trinity and ends in the Holy Trinity. The essence of Christian tradition is described by Saint Paul who declares that ". . . *God* chose you from the beginning to be saved by the sanctifying Spirit and by faith in the truth. Through the Gospel that we brought he called you to this so that you should share the glory of our Lord Jesus Christ" (Thes 2.13-14). Later on, the same Apostle proclaims more fully this Trinitarian kerygma upon which both the biblical and patristic tradition still rests. He writes to the Ephesians: "But now in Christ Jesus, you that used to be so far apart from us have been brought very close, by the blood of Christ. For he is peace between us, and has made the two into one and broken down the barrier which used to keep them apart, actually destroying in his own person the hostility caused by the rules and decrees of the Law. This was to create one single man in himself out of the two of them and by restoring peace through the cross, to unite them both in a single body and reconcile them with *God*. In his own person he killed the hostility. . . . Through him both of us have in the one Spirit our way to come to the Father" (Eph 2.13-18). From these two Pauline quotations, it becomes obvious the Trinitarian basis of the kerygma of salvation, which of course runs throughout patristic literature, the credal pronouncements and the liturgical prayers of the Church.

The authors of the books of the New Testament were conscious of their responsibility to give and share this message of salvation with the people of God. They fully realized that "Every good gift and every perfect gift is from above and comes down from the Father of the lights . . ." as Saint James writes (Jas 1.17). And Saint John emphasizes that he is the disciple who testifies "of these things and wrote these things; and we know that his testimony is true . . ." and he frankly confesses that he could not write all that Jesus did, for "if they should be written every one, I suppose that even the world itself could not contain the books that sould be written" (Jn 21.24-25).

This written and unwritten testimony for which Saint John speaks about has already become the apostolic tradition upon which the life of the Church would be built and would be tested. Saint Paul who did not belong to the immediate grouping of the first twelve Apostles is even more conscious of his duty to proclaim Christ's kerygma and he is compelled to write:

> Not that I do boast of preaching the gospel, since it is a duty which has been laid on me; I should be punished if I did not preach it! If I had chosen this work myself, I might have been paid for it, but as I have not, it is a responsibility which has been put into my hands. Do you know what my reward is? It is this: in my preaching to be able to offer the gospel freely, and not insist on the rights which the gospel gives me (1 Cor 9.16-18).

Saint Paul is so consistent and so faithful to this gospel that he admonishes the Galatians that even if an angel from heaven preaches another gospel to them than that which he had preached to them he is to be condemned. And he pleads: "If any man preach any other gospel to you than you have received (παρ' ὃ παρελάβετε) let him be condemned" (Gal 1.8-9). Speaking about the sacrament of Eucharist, Saint Paul writes: "For I have received (παρέλαβον) of the Lord that which also delivered (ὃ καὶ παρέδωκα)" (1 Cor 11.23). Again speaking about the death, burial and the resurrection of Christ, he writes: "For I delivered to you (παρέδωκα γὰρ ὑμῖν) first of all that which I also received (ὃ καὶ παρέλαβον)" (1 Cor 15.3). He is absolutely sure that the Thessalonians received (παραλαβόντες λόγον ἀκοῆς) the word of God from him and not the word of men (1 Thes 2.13). Also well-known is his strong admonition to the Thessalonians: "Brethren, stand fast and hold the traditions (τὰς παραδόσεις ἃς ἐδιδάχθητε) which you have been taught, whether by word or our epistle" (1 Thes 2.15).

One does not need to be a New Testament scholar in order to realize that during the apostolic years we have already a set of certain doctrines, creeds, liturgical practices, which originated from our Lord himself and which the Apostles felt obliged to expound, present, interpret and preserve not as dead pronouncements and ritualistic ceremonials, but as their own living experience and of the whole Church as well.

The pivotal question which arises immediately is how the transition from the biblical era to the patristic period took place. As we have already noted, we do not have here a legal transmission, or an abrupt chronological stepping-stone to another completely foreign period in the life of the Church. Here we have a smooth, continuous historical advancement of the same ecclesiological reality, that is, we have again the Holy Trinity acting in the Church (after the Apostles' departure from this world). That is, we have again the life in truth, in full power, the life of perfection and sanctification, to use two words used in *Didache*.[25]

Speaking of the *Didache*, one might be justified in saying that it is the first written document after the books of the New Testament (written circa the end of the first century A. D. or in the first quarter of the second century) which links the New Testament period with the patristic. *The Lord's Teaching to the Gentiles through the Twelve Apostles* or Διδαχὴ τοῦ Κυρίου διὰ τῶν Δώδεκα Ἀποστόλων τοῖς Ἔθνεσιν,[26] is a compilation or a compendium of precepts of morality, organization problems, liturgical functions and simple dogmatic pronouncements and as such it shows the organic, functional and liturgical unity of the Apostolic era, with the subapostolic generation preceeding it and with the patristic period of the Church following it. This is why it enjoyed great esteem among the Fathers. Saint Athanasios, although not classifying it among the canonical books of the New Testament, says that the Fathers permit its reading especially for the purpose of instructing the catechumens.[27]

But the first early patristic document which offers to us the patristic concept of tradition is the letter of Saint Clement, bishop of Rome at the last quarter of the first century A. D. He combines the notions of ecclesiastical discipline, apostolic succession, the authority of the Scriptures and the authority of the Fathers, who here are not others than the "God appointed" clergy. The Corinthians are reminded (1) that they must not transgress God's *"appointed rule of his service"*;[28] (2) that the Apostles knew through our Lord Jesus Christ that there would be a struggle over the name of the bishop's office and therefore "provided a continuance, that if these should fall asleep, other approved men should succeed to their ministration. . . ."[29] These have been appointed by the Apostles or their successors, "with the consent of the whole Church."[30] (3) The Scriptures—which the Corinthians should already have read— "are true" and "were given through the Holy Spirit."[31] (4) The Lord's Gospel was received by the Apostles and the Apostles gave it to their successors in order to proclaim the glad tidings of the salvation of mankind. We think that it is worthy of quoting this whole paragraph, for it describes in the most brilliant manner the organic connection and close unity of the historical on-going of the Christian Church in terms of biblical and patristic involvement. "The Apostles," Saint Clement writes, "received the Gospel for us from the Lord Jesus Christ; Jesus Christ was sent forth from God. So then Christ is from God, and the Apostles are from Christ. Both therefore came of the will of God in the appointed order. Having therefore a charge, and having been fully assured through the resurrection of our Lord Jesus Christ and confirmed in the word of God with full assurance of the Holy Ghost, they went forth with the glad tidings that the kingdom of God should come. So preaching everywhere in country and town, they appointed their first-fruits, when they have proved them by the Spirit, to be bishops and deacons unto them that should believe. . . ."[32]

Thus we can see here the whole linear horizontal on-going of the history of salvation. First the Holy Trinity as the source of our salvation and the fountain of the kerygma of the New Testament; then the Apostles and thirdly the Fathers of the Church, or "the gift, kerygma, application."[33] In other words, we have here the whole scheme of salvation in Christ, the fullness of revelation and the totality of apostolic and patristic tradition.

Saint Ignatios, the bishop of Antioch, who suffered martyrdom in Rome (circa 98-117), considers the written Gospel as archives (ἀρχεῖα), that is, historical documents which describe the advent of Christ, but at the same time, in passing, he seems to ignore the written Gospel, for he declares: "But as for me, my archives (ἀρχεῖ) is Jesus Christ; the inviolable archive is his cross and his death and his resurrection, and faith through him. . . ."[34] Then, however, he proceeds to justify the Gospel by the texts of the Old Testament, or rather he tries to encompass the Old Testament history with the New Testament testimony and with the experience of the Church. He writes:

> The priests likewise were good, but better is the high-priest to whom is committed the holy of holies: for him alone are committed the hidden things of God; he himself being the door of the Father, through which Abraham and Isaak and Jacob enter in, and the Prophets and the Apostles and the whole Church; all these combine in the unity of God. But the Gospel has a singular preeminence in the advent of the Savior, even our Lord Jesus Christ, and his passion and resurrection. For the beloved Prophets in their preaching pointed to him; but the Gospel is the completion of immortality. . . .[35]

Again speaking about the teaching of the Gospel, Saint Ignatios declares that "It is better to keep silence and to be, than to talk and not to be. . . . He that truly possesses the word of Jesus is able to hear unto His silence that he may be perfect; that through his speech he may act and through his silence he may be known. . . ."[36] Saint Ignatios gives us the wholeness of and the fullness of the divine plan of salvation which begins from the Old Testament times and at the same time he presents the totality of Christian Tradition which has its roots in the Old Testament, but it culminates in the apostolic tradition and in the life of the Church. Tradition is seen by him as a manifestation of the unity of God and this is why he declares the secret or the silent approach to tradition. Saint Ignatios sets the prerequisite for knowing and living the tradition of the Church and this is a silent or mystical study of the teaching of the Gospel. Tradition should not be spoken of always. We must listen in silence the word of God and be his temple so he may live in us. Thus in Saint Ignatios the concept of tradition becomes both mystical or silent and a dynamic, active reality which is lived by the people of God in the Church, "which breathes incorruption."[37]

Saint Polycarp, bishop of Smyrna, who was a contemporary of Saint Ignatios and who probably was a disciple of Saint John the Evangelist,[38] in his letter to the Phillippians defines the concept of Tradition as the faith of our Lord[39] or as the testimony of the cross,[40] as the Lord's *commandments* to the Apostles who preached the *Gospel*.[41] Saint Polycarp praises the Phillippians for the "steadfast root" of their faith "which was famed from primitive times, abides until now and bears fruit unto our Lord Jesus Christ." He also makes clear that those who pervert the words of the Lord are the first-born of Satan and he points to the vain doing of the many and their false teachings which are in abysmal conflict and contrast with the word which was delivered unto us from the beginning (ἐπὶ τὸν ἐξ ἀρχῆς ἡμῖν παραδοθέντα λόγον).[42]

Eusebios the bishop of Caesarea in Palestine and the Father of Church History writing about Hegesippos, the famous Hellenistic Jew and ecclesiastical writer who visited Rome in the middle of the second century, informs us that he has made use of Hegesippos' tradition quoting details as to the apostolic age. For Hegesippos, Eusebios continues, "collected his material in five books, giving in the simplest style of writing the unerring tradition of the apostolic preaching" (τὴν ἀπλανῆ παράδοσιν τοῦ ἀποστολικοῦ κηρύγματος).[43] Hegesippos had a deep concern for *the true doctrine* preached in the church of Corinth (till the time Primus was bishop of this great apostolic Church) and he explains "how when travelling as far as Rome he mingled with many bishops and that he found the same doctrine among them all." Speaking about the apostolic succession of the bishops, he comments that in each list and in each city things are as the law, the prophets, and the Lord preach.[44]

Saint Justin the philosopher and martyr, who was probably beheaded in Rome (circa 165), repeatedly claims that the teaching of his own and his contemporary Christians is based absolutely on the teaching which was delivered and taught by the Apostles and their successors. "We have learned (from our tradition) that God has no need of material offering from men. . . . We have been taught and firmly believe that he (God) accepts only those who imitate the good things which are his. . . ."[45] Saint Justin again and again calls Jesus Christ Teacher (Διδάσκαλον) and he says that "We are sure that all things taught by him are so . . ."[46] and he presents evidence to the Roman emperors "that the things we say as disciples of Christ and of the prophets before him, are the only truths, and older than all the writers who have lived, and we ask to be accepted, not because we say the same things as they do, but because we are speaking the truth—that Jesus Christ alone was really begotten as Son of God, being his word and first-begotten and power, and becoming man by his will he taught us these things for the reconciliation and resotration of the human race. . . ."[47] He proclaims also without any hesitation that the Christian teaching (or the apostolic teaching)[48] is superior of any human philosophy,[49] for actually Christ's teaching "is the only reliable and profitable philosophy."[50] Saint Justin believes that the Christian teaching is divine,[51] and he is ready at the same time to accept the fact that there are people who claim that they are Christians and use the name of Christ, but in reality they are heretics and schismatics (the Gnostics). Thus he is forced to make the distinction between the false teaching of the Gnostics and the true and pure teaching of Christ whose disciple he himself is.[52]

It is most interesting to note here that Saint Justin links the already existing Christian traditional teaching not only with the true faith but also with the true liturgical praxis of the Church. It is significant, we think, that when he is referring to the eucharist he always says that the Lord himself delivered (παρέδωκεν) and the Christians received (παρέλαβον) the eucharistic practice during which the bread and the wine offered by the people become with the prayer of the bishop or the priest the body and the blood of Christ.[53]

Speaking of the liturgical character of the apostolic and patristic tradition, one must not fail to mention Saint Hippolytos' book on the *Apostolic Tradition*, which embraces the liturgical functions of the Church of the early three Christian centuries. (Hippolytos suffered martyrdom around 235 A.D.) This apostolic and patristic tradition "which has continued up to now,"[54] Hippolytos finds needful to pass on to posterity because of the lapse and error which occurred in his times in the church of Rome. In addition, he believes that the Holy Spirit will supply perfect grace especially to those who rule the Church, who of course should transmit and keep aright this tradition.[55] In one of the prayers for the ordination of the bishop, which Saint Hippolytos preserved for us, one can see that the Holy Spirit keeps the order of the apostolic succession and the apostolic tradition and thus one can detect here the *vertical* or *horizontal* plane or line of Christian tradition, which becomes an instrument or a gift of the Holy Spirit, receiving its fullness from above and revealing continuously the divine energies of the Holy Spirit, who is a ceaseless

guide and force of all the ecclesiastical life and teaching. This important
ordination prayer is as follows:

> Do Thou pour forth that power which is from Thee, of the princely
> Spirit (τὸ Ἡγεμονικὸν Πνεῦμα) which Thou didst deliver to Thy be-
> loved Servant Jesus Christ, which he bestowed on Thy Holy Apostles
> who established in every place the Church which hallows Thee, to
> the glory and the praise of Thy name: Grant it, O Father that knowest
> the heart of all, upon this servant whom hast chosen for the
> episcopate to feed Thy holy flock. . . .[56]

In connection with this liturgical character of the patristic tradition
we must also mention the celebrated 27th chapter of Saint Basil's treatise
On the Holy Spirit. Praying towards the East, the words of the invocation over the eucharistic bread and cup of wine, the blessing of the water
of baptism and of the oil of chrism, the renunciation of Satan and his
angels, the sign of the cross, the custom of standing for prayer on Sundays (the day of the Resurrection) three immensions in baptism, etc., all
these, Saint Basil writes, "we have received delivered to us 'in a mystery'
(1 Cor 2.7) by the Tradition of the Apostles."[57] "Does not this," Saint
Basil asks with candor, "come from that unpublished and secret teaching
which our fathers guarded in a silence out of the reaches of curious med-
dling and inquisitive investigation? Well had they learnt the lesson that
the awful dignity of the mysteries is best preserved by silence. . . ."[58]
And just as Moses acted correctly in not making all the parts of the tabernacle open to everyone, "in the same manner the *Apostles* and the *Fathers*
laid down laws for the Church from the beginning and thus guarded the
awful dignity of the mysteries in secrecy and silence, for what is bruited
abroad at random among the common folk is no mystery at all. This is
the reason for our tradition of unwritten precepts and practices, that the
knowledge of our dogmas may not become neglected and condemned
by the multitude through familiarity. " 'Dogma' and 'kerygma' are two
distinct things; the former is observed in silence; the latter is proclaimed to all the world. One form of this silence is the obscurity employed
in Scripture, which makes the meaning of 'dogmas' difficult to be
understood for the very advantage of the reader. . . ."[59]

Aside from the liturgical asepcts of the apostolic and patristic tradition (for which Saint Basil proclaims their unity and close relation and
continuity), this whole chapter (27th) of the treatise *On the Holy Spirit*
poses serious problems which demand closer attention and study.

First of all, Saint Basil seems to distinguish between "dogma" and "kerygma." These two terms should not be explained in the semantics of the contemporary theological parlance. Actually, "dogma" in Saint Basil's language does not mean a definition of doctrine of the Church. As Father Georges Florovsky remarked in his excellent monograph on *The Function of Tradition in the Ancient Church,* "the concept and the term 'dogma' was not yet fixed by that time — it was not yet a term with a strict and exact connotation."[60] "Dogmata," for Saint Basil meant at that time τὰ ἄγραφα τῶν ἐθῶν, the "unwritten customs," that is "the whole structure of liturgical and sacramental life."[61] In other words, Saint Basil speaks of the silent and secret functions of the liturgical life of the Church which were not open to the uninitiated. The term "kerygma," which is of New Testament origin and denotes precisely the preaching and the declaration of the Christian faith, on an authoritative basis, is proclaimed freely and openly "to all the world."[62] However, in the early period of the Church, these "dogmata" could become and be transformed into "kerygmata," as Saint Basil himself does in this treatise *On the Holy Spirit,* himself revealing some of these secret "dogmata" or liturgical customs. In any case, included among the unpublished "dogmata" were the baptismal creeds and the doxology of the Holy Trinity.[63] Faith and liturgical functions were intermingled and infused into each other, and Saint Basil was aware of the fact that the secret "dogmata," this tradition of unwritten precepts and practices[64] leads in reality to the recognition that salvation is established through the Father and the Son and the Holy Spirit, which is the doctrine taught at our baptism;[65] besides "in what way are we saved? Plainly because we were regenerated through the grace given in our baptism."[66]

Saint Basil also makes a distinction between the written teaching (ἔγγραφος διδασκαλία) and the unwritten teaching (ἄγραφος διδασκαλία) or the unpublished and secret teaching (σιωπωμένη καὶ μυστικὴ παράδοσις).[67] He does not believe that the tradition of the apostles was not all delivered in written form. He asks for instance: "And as to the customs of baptism from what Scripture do we derive the renunciation of satan and his angels?"[68] He claims "that time will fail him if he attempts to recount the unwritten mysteries of the Church...." In attacking those who reject the authority of the unwritten tradition (which he considers to have the same force ἅπερ ἀμφότερα τὴν ἰσχὺν ἔχει πρὸς τὴν εὐσέβειαν[69] with the written tradition or the Scripture), he writes: "The one aim of the whole band of opponents and enemies of the 'sound doctrine' (1 Tim 1.10) is to shake down the foundation of the faith of Christ by leveling apostolic tradition to the ground, and utterly destroying it. So like debtors—of course bona fide debtors—they clamor for written proof, and reject as worthless the unwritten tradition of the Fathers. But we will not slacken in our defense of the truth. . . ."[70] This unwritten tradition, which has to do not only with the liturgical functions of the Church but also with the most important commitment of the neophytes and of all Christians, namely the confession (especially at the baptismal font) of the Holy Trinity, is a mystery which a man uninitiated into the faith is not able to comprehend as such and he might easily come to scorn or desecrate it.

Here the "disciplina arcani," or the discipline of secrecy comes into focus. It was a practice of the ancient Church to keep in secrecy the Creed, or certain functions of the liturgical life of the Church, so that the infidel, or even the heretics could not profane them.

We have already mentioned the "silent" teaching of Saint Ignatios.[71] Clement of Alexandria in his *Stromata*[72] speaks of the unwritten and written teaching or the blessed and secured (ἀδιάδραστος) Tradition and the secret, veiled or hidden truth of the Christian religion.[73] Saint Cyril of Jerusalem admonishes the catechumens "to tell nothing to a stranger" about what their teachers have said.[74] Sozomen in his *History* even avoids completely the quotation of the Nicene Creed "which only the initiated and the mystagogues have the right to recite and hear."[75] Also in the West both Rufinus and Saint Augustine avoided writing down the Creed on paper. It must be made clear, however, that the secret discipline was not a kind of an exclusive structure of kerygmata or dogmas kept secretly and in silence among certain "elite" or super-Christians. This would be a sheer heresy, since the gnostics claimed such an exclusive "aristocratic" privilege of having received a secret tradition from God exclusively revealed to their selected and most perfect group. So the terms σιγή, ἡσυχία (Saint Ignatios), ἄγραφος διδασκαλία, σιωπωμένη μυστικὴ παράδοσις (Saint Basil), μυστήριόν σου γὰρ παραδίδομεν (Saint Cyril of Jerusalem) ἀδιάδραστος καὶ μακαρία παράδοσις, or ἐγκεκαλυμμένη καὶ ἐπικεκρυμμένη ἀλήθεια (Clement of Alexandria) have the meaning of the "mysterious," the "sacramental" and the "ecclesiological." There are those who have been initiated into the life of the Church; by the sacrament of baptism they have become children of God and through the holy eucharist they have been united with God. Only in the Church of Christ where the Holy Spirit abides, the truth is revealed in a mysterious way and this fullness of truth is lived and experienced.

Contemporary Orthodox theologians have suggested that in order to understand more fully the concept or the doctrine of the patristic tradition in particular or the concept of Tradition in general we might speak of Tradition (with capital T) and about traditions (with small t)—Παράδοσις καὶ παραδόσεις.[76] It has been suggested that the whole historical scheme of Tradition should be described as follows: tradition (with small t) which is the oral transmission of the divine revelation which preceded the Scripture; then Scripture (with capital S), the scripture (with small s) which include all the forms of the written expression, interpretation and formulation of the received Truth; and finally Tradition (with capital T) which is the apostolic and ecclesiastical tradition and is absolutely necessary for the salvation of mankind[77] (παράδοσις—Γραφή—γραφή—Παράδοσις).

It is true that these diagrams do help to understand the intricate historical problems concerning Tradition. And it is true that this approach solves many a problem as far as the nature and the structure of Tradition is concerned. One, however, must be cautious not to over-stretch this kind of interpretation not only because it leads to dichotomy and breaking of horizontal and vertical planes of Tradition, but at the same time it introduces two roads or two ways in the historical on-going of the Church. Tradition (with capital T) and traditions (with small t) are very hard to separate and distinguish in the life of the Church, at least from the first and quick glance. Personally, we do accept this interpretation, with the understanding that both Tradition and traditions lead to each other and none can survive without each other. In fact, the distinction of Tradition and traditions is not foreign to the Fathers of the Church. Saint Photios reminds us that there is a line which could be drawn between the ecclesiastical faith, whose rejection leads to death, and the ecclesiastical customs which might be different from place to place. Unity is indispensable to the essential teachings of Tradition, whereas in secondary matters change and variation do not inhibit the unifying grace of the Holy Spirit.[78] The Patriarchs of the East writing to the English Non-Jurors in 1723, emphasized the common grounds of the faith and the unanimity demanded for the doctrines (this term in the contemporary sense) of faith, but they were willing to accept the historical existence of the variations of ecclesiastical customs, etc.[79] Classical in this case is Saint Irenaios' rebuke of Pope Victor who wanted to cut off from the common unity the dioceses of all Asia for refusing to follow the Roman customs on the celebration of Easter and of fasting ". . . the disagreement in the fast confirms our agreement in the faith."[80]

The men who really set the foundations concerning the interpretation of the patristic tradition are Saint Irenaios, Tertullian and Saint Athanasios. We do know that the favorite phrase of Saint Irenaios is the

rule of faith (κανὼν ἀληθείας) or regula veritatis. This rule, or manifestation or preaching of truth, is nothing else in reality but the witness of
the Apostles and their successors in the Church. He writes: "Now the
Church, although scattered over the whole civilized world to the end of
the earth, received from the Apostles and their disciples its faith. . . .
Having received this preaching and this faith, as I have said, the Church,
although scattered in the whole world, carefully preserves it, as if living
in one house. . . . For the languages of the world are different, but the
meaning of the tradition is one and the same. . . . But as God's creation,
the sun is one and the same in the whole world, so also the preaching
of truth shines everywhere, and illumines all men who wish to come to
the knowledge of truth. . . ."[81] He likes to remind us that "The Lord
of all gave to his apostles the power of the gospel, and by them we also
have learned the truth . . ."[82] and that "tradition . . . comes down from
the apostles and is guarded by the succession of the elders . . ."[83] or
"the tradition of the Apostles, made clear in all the world, can be clearly
seen in every church by those who wish to behold the truth. We can
enumerate those who were established by the apostles as bishops in the
churches, and their successors down to our time. . . ."[84] Binding
together apostolic succession and apostolic tradition, Saint Irenaios claims
that "In this very order and succession the apostolic tradition of the
Church and the preaching of the truth has come down to us. This is a
full demonstration that it is one and the same life-giving faith which has
been preserved in the Church from the apostles to the present, and is
handed in truth."[85]

Saint Irenaios, in pressing the point on apostolic tradition and
apostolic succession, seeks to combat the Gnostics who claimed that they
have received the true gnosis directly from God. But the gnostic speculations lack precisely the most important and essential qualification, that
is, the charisma of truth which comes only through the Apostles and their
successors. "Wherefore," Saint Irenaios writes, "it is incumbent to obey
the presbyters who are in the Church, those as I have shown who possess
the succession from the Apostles; those who, together with the succession of the episcopate, have received the certain gift of truth, according
to the good pleasure of the Father. . . ."[86] Writing to Florinus (a Mon-
tanist presbyter in Rome) he reminds him, "These opinions, O Florinus,
that I may speak sparingly, do not belong to sound doctrine. These opinions are inconsistent with the Church, and bring those who believe in
them into the greatest impiety. . . . These opinions, those who were
presbyters before us, they who accompanied the apostles, did not hand
on to you. . . ."[87]

From these extensive quotations it is apparent that this great Father of the third century had placed the concept of Tradition in its proper place. He accuses the gnostics of mishandling and misinterpreting the Scripture because they try to study it apart from the community of the Church, whose unity is expressed in apostolic succession and in the soundness and the catholicity of the Christian orthodox doctrine, as preserved by the successors of the Apostles. Father Florovsky has already mentioned the contribution of Saint Irenaios in showing that the gnostics re-arranged the Scriptural evidence on a pattern which is quite alien to the Scripture itself.[88] It might be added that Saint Irenaios has established the close links between Scripture and patristic tradition by pointing to their intrinsic historical continuity and by showing that arbitrary interpretations of the Scripture are a sin towards man's own self, disrespect to the Holy Trinity, as well as self-incrimination and resistance to and refusal of one's personal salvation.[89] Tradition, therefore, in the eyes of Saint Irenaios has a profound soteriological meaning and those who violate its principles are bound to eternal punishment.

Tertullian, before he cut off his relations with the catholic Church, was deeply interested in the concept of Tradition. He writes: "Every sort of thing must necessarily be referred back to its origin. Therefore the churches, although they are so many and so great, comprise but the one primitive Church, founded by the Apostles, from which they all spring. In this way all are primitive, and all are apostolic, whilst they are all in one unity by their peaceful communion and title of brotherhood and bond of hospitality, privileges which no other rule directs than the one tradition of the selfsame rule of faith. . . ."[90] Here again it is obvious that Tertullian realizes the value of Tradition and its function as a continuous on-going of the life of the Church. All and everything the Church teaches are primitive and apostolic because their origin and foundation are primitive and apostolic.

But the locus classicus of patristic tradition is given by Saint Athanasios: "Let us look," he writes, "at that very tradition, teaching and faith of the Catholic Church from the very beginning, which the Lord gave (ἔδωκεν), the Apostles preached (ἐκήρυξαν), and the Fathers preserved (ἐφύλαξαν). Upon this the Church is founded (τεθεμελίωται)."[91]

Saint John Chrysostom also finds a close bond between the Church and Tradition: "Therefore we must consider Traditions of the Church trustworthy. It is Tradition, seek no more."[92] And Saint John of Damascus writes: "Moreover, faith is twofold. For 'faith comes by hearing' (Rom 10.17). For by hearing the divine Scripture we believe in the teaching of the Holy Spirit. The same is perfected by all things enjoined

by Christ, believing in work, cultivating piety, and doing the commands
of him who restored us. For he that believes not according to the tradition of the catholic Church, or who has intercourse with the devil through
strange works, is an unbeliever. But again, 'faith is the substance of things
hoped for, the evidence of things not seen' (Heb 11.1), or undoubting
and unambiguous hope alike of what God has promised us and of the
good issue of our prayers. The first, therefore, belongs to our will, while
the second is of the gifts of the Holy Spirit."[93]

Saint John of Damascus epitomizes here the patristic concept of Tradition and shows that both the Scripture and the patristic tradition are
in contact with and come from the Holy Spirit which is the source of
all gifts.

However Saint John, writing somewhat later about the dormition of
the Virgin Mary and describing her death and her burial in detail, says
that when the disciples of Christ opened her casket they did not find
her body but only the clothes in which she had been wrapped. Then he
continues to say that this story is not found in the holy and divine-inspired
Scripture but it has been received from the ancient and true tradition.
"Τῇ μὲν ἁγίᾳ καὶ θεοπνεύστῳ Γραφῇ οὐκ ἐμφέρεται τὰ κατὰ τὴν τελευτὴν
τῆς ἁγίας Θεοτόκου Μαρίας ἐξ ἀρχαίας δὲ καὶ ἀληθεστάτης παραδόσεως
παρειλήφαμεν. . . ."[94] The question which may naturally arise now is
whether in this great Father of the Church we face a new concept of
Tradition, that is a Tradition which is something different from the Scripture. Of course, if one studies carefully the previous quotations from his
book *Exposition of the Orthodox Faith*, he will find that in Saint John's
mind Scripture and Tradition are not two different things. Both are gifts
of the Holy Spirit. Saint John realizes without any doubt that the Scriptures do not contain all the events and facts relating to Christ and his
Mother. Thus Tradition becomes a supplementary to the biblical story
of salvation. To be sure, Scripture has in itself everything needed for
the salvation of mankind. But the Fathers of the Church preserved for
posterity events and stories of which some might have importance for
our salvation, and others might have importance for our information or
edification. Again everything goes back to the primitive apostolic tradition and thus only through the scope and the light of this apostolic tradition all sacred history should be viewed and comprehended.

One of the most important aspects as far as the patristic tradition
is concerned is the concept of authority in and about the Fathers of the
Church. Authority, ἐξουσία or αὐθεντία in Greek and auctoritas in Latin,
is of biblical origin. The absolute authority (*exousia*) belongs to the Lord
himself for as Saint Matthew says: "For he [Christ] taught them as one

having authority.''[95] This exousia, which means both authority and power, does not enforce obedience though external coercion. It is the power of the Holy Trinity which gives strength to the Apostles and their successors to continue the life of faith and to proclaim the glad tidings. This is the authentia of the Church.[96] The sixth canon of the Council of Sardica (343) speaks of the authentia of the bishops which should not be violated.[97] Pope Hormisdas (523), in his letter to Epiphanios, assures him that the Council of Chalcedon with its own authority expounded and confirmed the previous Ecumenical Councils.[98] Then the pseudonymous titles of the *Didache*, the *Didascalia Apostolorum*, the *Apostolic Constitutions* and the *Apostolic Canons, the Apostolic Tradition* of Saint Hippolytos and the *Demonstration of the Apostolic Teaching* of Saint Irenaios are ample examples of the authority even the names of the Apostles referred most frequently to the authority of the Bible, but not merely as supreme locus theologicus but rather as spiritual nourishment and as starting point leading to full communion with God,[99] to a real way of life in Christ and through Christ. Thus for the immediate successors of the Apostles and the later Fathers the Scriptures are not above and beyond the Church. There are not two sources of authority. For the early Christian Fathers the Pauline concept of recapitulation (ἀνακεφαλαίωσις) or the doctrine of (καινὴ κτίσις) were historical events which they experienced in the Church and through the Church. Moreover, the Fathers were not merely exegetes and interpreters of the Scripture. They were leaders and they were conscious of their calling and mission. Even their enemies realized their leading role and they called them Fathers. Saint Polycarp of Smyrna was called "the Father of the Christians" by the pagan adversaries who led him to his martyrdom.[100] One might rightly say that the Fathers derive their authority from the Holy Spirit who lives in the Church and from the self-consciousness that they are instruments of the Holy Trinity. Reading the Fathers, one realizes that in their writings, though they may often not be of superior or even tolerable philological or aesthetic character, there flows an inner power, an assurance which is not of this world. Thus, the early successors of the Apostles did not use only the Scripture. They were ready to refer to their predecessors as sources of prestige and inspiration. Saint Polycarp, for instance, collected the letters of Saint Ignatios and forwarded them to the Church of Philippi. He knew and he used the first letter of Saint Clement of Rome. Later Saint Irenaios, in combating the Gnostics, quoted heavily from previous patristic texts (Clement of Rome, Saint Polycarp of Smyrna, Saint Justin the Martyr, Saint Ignatios, Theophilos of Antioch). *The Appeal of the Fathers* was a common process and function

in the course of the patristic tradition.[101] Even Saint Basil appeals to
Saint Irenaios, Saint Clement of Rome, Dionysios of Rome and of Alexandria. Saint Athanasios[102] and Saint Basil[103] use the term "Fathers of
the Church" referring collectively to the Fathers present at the First
Ecumenical Council of Nicaea (325 A. D.). It is worthy of special note
that at the Council of Ephesos the representatives of the Church of Antioch presented a dossier which included citations from Saint Ignatios,
Saint Irenaios, Saint Hippolytos, Saint Methodios. It also seems established that Cyril and the representatives of the Alexandrian side presented
a similar dossier with citations from early Fathers.[104]

It has been suggested by Professor Robert Wilken, in his learned article, "Tradition, Exegesis and the Christological Controversies,"[105] that
both Cyril and Nestorios each followed his own view and understanding
of theological tradition. Each one had behind him his own theological
background which could not be sustained on the common tradition of
the Church which both they invoked. It is true that Saint Cyril was a
student of the "School of Alexandria" and Nestorios belonged to the
"School of Antioch." This does not mean, however, that they were unfamiliar with the catholic tradition of the Church. Saint Cyril appeals
most of the times to the Fathers of the First Eumenical Council (Nicea,
325), that is to the universal and approved Tradition of the Church. The
dossier of patristic citations submitted to the Council of Ephesos (431)
by Peter the presbyter of the Church of Alexandria includes references
to Julius I, the bishop of Rome, Saint Cyprian, Saint Ambrose, Saint
Gregory the Theologian, Saint Gregory of Nyssa, Saint Basil the Great,
Attikos, bishop of Constantinople, and of course there are plentiful
references to Nestorios.[106]

Similarly, Nestorios himself also appeals to the First Ecumenical Council of Nicaea (325) and in his *Bazaar of Heracleids*, which constitutes his
Apology, he seems familiar with the Cappadocians and the Alexandrian
theologians as well as of those of the West.[107] In that sense both Cyril
and Nestorios realized the gravity and the seriousness of their argumentation and both tried hard to prove that their teachings were not simply
"provincial" but catholic and ancient. . . . The failure of Nestorios does
not lie on the fact that he was a prejudiced and unrevokable fanatic of
the School of Antioch. His great mistake was that being influenced by
the cataphatic theology of the School of Antioch and its great teachers
(especially Theodore of Mopsuestia) he saw the Incarnation in categories
of human exigencies. And more especially, as I have already pointed
out,[108] Nestorios' road to condemnation was due to the fact that he not
only looked at the term *theotokos* as a Trinitarian term, as Wilken[109]

rightly suggests, but even more, this Trinitarian approach was based on poor theology. His whole concept of God and his essence lacked the apophatic insight of the catholic theology. Nestorios broke the continuity of the patristic tradition in so far as he missed the totality and the fullness of the Christian doctrine of God and his relation with man and the world.

Thus Wilken's evaluation of the christological controversy of the fifth century, though reasonable and comfortable as it may seem, underestimates the impact of the doctrine of Tradition on both schools and overestimates Nestorios' ability to perceive through patristic tradition the dangerous consequences of his erroneous presuppositions and orientation.[110]

We have reached the end of this study. We have allowed the Fathers of the Church to speak for themselves. We have presented their opinions oftentimes without comment and discussion purposely, so that the Fathers may speak themselves.

The most critical question which might be asked after this study of the patristic sources, is whether we do really have a patristic concept of Tradition at all. As the books of the Scripture were written because of the needs and the circumstances which arose in the times of the authors, the same could be said for the Fathers of the Church. They wrote, not for the purpose of intellectual exercise, nor because of aesthetic inclinations, nor out of worldly aims. They wrote, in accordance to their understanding of their mission, in order to teach, edify and save souls for the sake of Christ. So we must frankly admit that there is no conceptualized formulation or any development of any theory among the Fathers concerning Tradition. When they spoke about Tradition, they did so because circumstances demanded it, as for instance the combat against heresies. One might say that they not only were thrilled about Tradition,[111] but that they felt and lived Tradition. Tradition for them was not the enumeration of quotations from the Scriptures or the previous Fathers; it was the offspring of the incarnation of the Word of God which took place in space and time. Thus Tradition was a continuous extension into history of the incarnation of the Son of God. They felt, at the same time, that they had to live under the continuous presence of the Holy Spirit because, as Saint Basil writes: "Through the Holy Spirit comes our restoration to paradise, our ascension into the kingdom of heaven, our return to the adoption of sons, our liberty to call God our Father, our being made partakers of the grace of Christ, our being called children of light, our sharing in eternal glory, and, in a word, our being brought into a state of all 'fullness of blessing' (Rom 15.29), both in this world and in the world to come. . . ."[112]

This is indeed a profound description of the role of the Holy Spirit in the life of the Church, a life which is not conditioned by human terms but by the work of the Holy Trinity itself. It is also a paradox, so to say, that the Fathers do not use the term Tradition (Παράδοσις) as might be expected. They appealed to the Scriptures, they appealed to the precedent Fathers and undisputably looked towards the roots and the primitive beginnings of the Church in order to derive arguments, strength and inspiration. But they never considered this appeal as a mechanical device, nor as a key to solve their problems. When, for instance, the decree of the Council of Chalcedon opened with the statement, "Following the Fathers . . ."[113] this does not imply any "refereence to some abstract tradition, in formulas and propositions," as Father Florovsky rightly points out.[114] "Following the Fathers . . ." is an experience of life, where faith and worship, the *lex credendi* and the *lex orandi* are integral part of the unanimous experience of the Church. This is why even the interpretation of the Scriptures is not considered an individual enterprise but rather an expression of the sensus catholicus or the ἐκκλησιαστικὸν φρόνημα,[115] of the ecclesiastical sense (ἐκκλησιαστικὴ διάνοια), to use Saint Athanasios' terminology, in contrast to "private opinions" of those who were outside the Church (the heretics).[116] This is why Saint Augustine writes: "I should not have believed the Gospel had not the authority of the catholic Church compelled me."[117]

Yes indeed the Fathers were great teachers; they were, as we have already mentioned, the eyes or the leaders of the Church, but at the same time they knew with humility that they were members of the Church of Christ, parts of the people of God, and therefore they knew that they should live and act in the light of the christological and pneumatological experience of the whole Church. Thus Saint Augustine quite humbly remarked: "As bishops we are pastors, but under the great Pastor we are sheep along with you; though in this place (cathedra) we are your teachers, under the one Master we are your fellow disciples in this school."[118] And Maximos the Confessor (c. 580-662) with humility stated: "I have no private teaching save the common doctrine of the catholic Church."[119] Or as it is said: "The Holy Spirit, who had wrought effectually in all the saints from the beginning of the world, and was afterwards sent to the Apostles by the Father . . . and after the Apostles to all believers in the holy catholic Church." Therefore ". . . the unvarying constancy and the unerring truth of Christian dogma . . . is guarded by the totality of the people of God. . . ."[120]

Here the famous dictum of Vincent Lerins has its proper place, "in ipsa item catholica ecclesia magnopere curandum est ut id teneamus quod ubique, quod semper, quod ab omnibus creditum est";[121] although one must remember that this maxim should not be taken numerically, but ecclesiologically. That is, patristic tradition is what always, everywhere and by everybody has been not merely transmitted, but lived as an experience of the Church, the true catholic Church (because there was a time, especially during the Arian controversy, when the Arian heresies prevailed over the minority of the Orthodox Fathers).

So the essence of the patristic tradition is not "Traditionalismus." Biblical formalism, intellecutal maximalism or philosophical exercises have no place in the Doctrine Patrum. Or as Anastasios Sinai (d. C. 700) put it, the Fathers neither interpret the Scripture nor taught in the Church in an Aristotelian way (ἀλιευτικῶς) or in Homeric way (ὁμηρικῶς), that is they excluded rationalism and mythologization; but they interpreted the Scripture and taught in the Church theologically (θεολογικῶς).[122] In other words, their whole life was a life of theology, a life of devotion. First they knew how to live according to Christ and then theologize. One might re-adapt the celebrated axiom, Primum vivere deinde philosophari, and say that the Fathers of the Church knew how to apply in their lives the maxim Primum vivere deinde theologizari, in the sense that although truth and theology and worship were their constant companions, their continuous aims, they sought them above all in the totality of the experience of the Church. They were men of action and contemplation, men of energy and thoughtfulness. Saint Augustine's motto, "In necessaris unitas, in dubiis libertas, in omnibus caritas," applies to most of them. This is why they did not develop a rigid and inflexible structure of private opinions and propositions. They were primarily interested in a constant dialogue with their own selves, then in a dialogue with their fellow-men, and finally they were interested in a dialogue with God.[123]

This is why Saint Neilos, the ascetic Father of the fifth century speaks about the "philosophy of the divine life" (φιλοσοφία θείου πολιτεύματος), or the spiritual philosophy (πνευματικὴ φιλοσοφία), or the lofty philosophy according to Christ (ἡ κατὰ Χριστὸν ὑψηλὴ φιλοσοφία).[124] He continuously speaks about the deep remembrance of Jesus the Lord of glory (βαθεῖα μνήμη—ἐνθύμησις—τοῦ Κυρίου τῆς δόξης), and blessed apathy which leads to the contemplation of God (μακαριωτάτη ἀπάθεια) and (θεωρία Θεοῦ).[125]

Saint Symeon the New Theologian, writes that if we want our deeds and our words to be in agreement with the Holy Fathers, then we must follow their example and then we shall reach some day the calm and undisturbed harbors of the eternal life, which is the life of the Holy

Trinity.[126]

Saint Gregory Palamas in summing up the patristic doctrine of Christian life suggests that the ultimate purpose of man's life is the θεοπτία, that is seeing God,[127] or to use Saint Gregory of Nyssa's words, man's life is strenuous, tiresome and endless escession towards God, *theosis* (θέωσις).[128]

So the patristic tradition is not a dead letter. It cannot be expressed fully in human terms and categories, since the Holy Spirit operates in it. No spiritual inertia, no passive toleration of the evil, not an exaggerated concern for history for the sake of an un-balanced historicism; these are not to be found in the Fathers. The patristic tradition, having its source and its roots in the Holy Trinity, is a dynamic process in history and above history, a genuine renewal of man, a mobile power, a vivifying light, which grants to man his absolute fulfilment in the pleroma of the Divine Energies of God.

NOTES

[1]Chapter 41.

[2]D. S. Balanos, *Πατρολογία* (Athens, 1930), p. 18; J. Quasten, *Patrology* (Utrecht-Brussels), 1, p. 10.

[3]Balanos, p. 19; Quasten, 1, p. 10. Van Campenhausen places the ending of the Patristic age at the fourth century, showing thus a complete misunderstanding of the work of the Holy Spirit in the Church. See his *The Fathers of the Greek Church* (New York, 1959), p. 11.

[4]On this see C. Bonis of the University of Athens who considers Chrysostomos Papadopoulos, late Archbishop of Athens (1868-1938) as a "Father" and "Teacher" of the Church. See *Ἐκκλησία*, 45 (1/15 Nov. 1968) 505.

[5]*Τοῦ ἐν ἁγίοις Πατρὸς ἡμῶν Ἰωάννου τοῦ Δαμασκηνοῦ ἐγκώμιον εἰς τὸν "Αγιον Ἰωάννην Χρυσόστομον*, PG 96.773.

[6]Symeon the New Theologian, *Κεφάλια πρακτικὰ καὶ θεολογικά*, 134, 145, 148; *Θεογνωσίας λόγος* 30, 1.

[7]Gregory of Nyssa, *Life of Moses*, ed. W. Jaeger and H. Musurillo (Leiden, 1964), p. 87.

[8]Niketas Stethatos, *Θεωρία εἰς τὸν παράδεισον*, ed. P. Chrestou (Thessalonike, 1957), p. 144.

[9]*Commentary*, chapter 41.

[10]Ibid.

[11]John Karmires, *Σύνοψις τῆς δογματικῆς διδασκαλίας τῆς Ὀρθοδόξου Καθολικῆς Ἐκκλησίας* (Athens, 1957), p. 12.

[12]English translation in *A Select Library of Nicene and Post-Nicene Fathers of the Christian Church*, second series. Ed. Philip Schaff and Henry Wage (Grand Rapids, 1956), 14, pp. 374-75.

[13]Gregory the Theologian, "The First Theological Oration," *The Library of Christian Classics*, ed. E. R. Hardy and C. C. Richardson, pp. 134-35; PG 36.25A.

[14]Ibid. p. 129.

[15]Theodore Stylianopoulos, "Historical Studies and Orthodox Theology on the Problem of History for Orthodoxy," *The Greek Orthodox Theological Review*, 12 (1967) 410.

[16]Ibid.

[17]Saint Athanasios, Βίος καὶ πολιτεία τοῦ ὁσίου πατρὸς ἡμῶν 'Αντωνίου, ch. 91. ΒΕΠΕΣ, 33, p. 55.

[18]Sergius Bulgakov, *The Church as Tradition* (New York, 1966), p. 4.

[19]T. J. Towers, "The Value of the Fathers," *The Church Quarterly Review*, 166 (July-Sept. 1965) 298.

[20]E. Flessman van-Leer, *Tradition and Scripture in Early Church* (Assen, 1954), pp. 92c.

[21]In *The Greek Orthodox Theological Review*, 11 (1965-1966) 188-99.

[22]Ibid.

[23]E. L. Fortin, "Clement of Alexandria and the Esoteric Tradition," *Studia Patristica* 7, pp. 3-26.

[24]Metropolitan Athenagoras, "Tradition and Traditions," *St. Vladimir's Seminary Quarterly* 7 (1963) 103.

[25]Ch. 10, 5.

[26]Quasten, pp. 29-30.

[27]Festal Letter No. 39, PG 26.1176.

[28]J. B. Lightfoot, *The Apostolic Fathers* (Grand Rapids, 1956), p. 30.

[29]Ibid. p. 32.

[30]Ibid.

[31]Ibid.

[32]Ibid. p. 31.

[33]Athenagoras, p. 104.

[34]"Letter to the Philadelphians," ch. 8; Lightfoot, p. 81.

[35]Ibid. ch. 9; Lightfoot, p. 81.

[36]"Letter to the Ephesians," ch. 15; Lightfoot, p. 67.

[37]Ibid. ch. 17; Lightfoot, p. 67.

[38]This information comes from Saint Irenaios and is presented for us by Eusebios in his E. H. 5, 20.

[39]"Letter to the Philippeans," ch. 4; Lightfoot, p. 96.

[40]Ibid. ch. 7; Lightfoot, p. 97.

[41]Ibid. ch. 6; Lightfoot, p. 97.

[42]Ibid. ch. 7; Lightfoot, p. 97.

[43]Eusebios, 6.8.

[44]Ibid. 4, 22.

[45]*First Apology*, ch. 10. See *Library of Christian Classics* 1, p. 247.

[46]Ibid. ch. 12; See also chps. 4, 6, 8, 13, 19, 21, 32, and *Second Apology*, chps. 2 and 4.

[47]*First Apology*, ch. 23; *Library*, 1, pp. 256-57.

[48]Ibid. ch. 53; *Library*, 1, p. 276.

[49]*Second Apology*, chps. 10 and 15.

[50]*Dialogue with Trypho*, ch. 8.

[51]Ibid. ch. 80.

[52]Ibid. ch. 35.

[53]*First Apology*, ch. 66; *Dialogue with Trypho*, ch. 41 and 70.

[54]*The Apostolic Tradition of Hippolytus*, ed. Gregory Dix (London, 1927), p. 2.

[55]Ibid.

[56]Ibid. pp. 4-5. This vertical plane or line, or this pheumatological character of Tradition, that is the close and straightward inter-connection of Tradition with the Holy Spirit is seen in Saint Hippolytos in chapters 3 and 35 of his *Apostolic Tradition*, where speaking about the liturgical sermons and instructions to the faithful, he points out that the teacher speaks with the grace of God and that the faithful "will be profited by what the *Holy Spirit will give him through the instructor* . . . therefore let everyone be zealous to go to the *church*, the place where the *Holy Spirit abounds* (or breaks forth and blooms)." Cf. Burton Scott Easton, *The Apostolic Tradition of Hippolytus* (Cambridge, 1934), p. 54.

[57]PG 32.188A-93A. For the English translation cf. *A Selected Library of Nicene and Post-Nicene Fathers of the Christian Church*, ed. Philip Schaff and H. Wage (Grand Rapids, 1956), 8, p. 41.

[58]Ibid. p. 42.

[59]Ibid.

[60]In *The Greek Orthodox Theological Review* 9 (1963-1964), 194.

[61]Ibid.

[62]*On the Holy Spirit*, p. 42. On the meaning and interpretation of the terms "dogma" and kerygma" cf. Dom. Odo Casel, *Das christliche Kultusmysterium* (Regensburg, 1932), pp. 105 ff., where there is a pertinent discussion of the mysterial or sacramental meanings of these terms. For a profound analysis of the relation between these terms cf. Vladimir Lossky, *Tradition and Traditions*. Cf. Leonid Ouspensky and Vladimir Lossky, *The Meaning of Icons*, tr. G. E. H. Palmer and E. Kadloubovsky, ed. Urs Grafverlag Olten (Boston, 1952), pp. 13-24.

[63]*On the Holy Spirit*, ch. 10. *Select Library*, 8, p. 17.

[64]Ibid. ch. 25; *Select Library*, 8, p. 42.

[65]Ibid. ch. 10; *Select Library*, 8, p.17

[66]Ibid.

[67]Ibid. ch. 27; *Select Library*, 8, pp. 41-42.

[68]Ibid.; *Select Library*, 8, p. 42.

[69]Ibid.; *Select Library*, 8, p. 41.

[70]Ibid. ch 10; *Select Library*, 8, pp. 16-17.

[71]*Letter to the Ephesians*, ch. 15.

[72]Book 1, ch. 1.

[73]Ibid. Discussion concerning the concept of the "Esoteric Tradition" is found in the most informative article of E. L. Fortin, "Clement of Alexandria and the Esoteric Tradition," in *Studia Patristica*, vol. 9, pp. 41 ff., with the most recent bibliography on the subject. It is worthy to note that Fortin does discuss pertinenty Prof. Hanson's theory on the Philonic origin of Clement's concept on Tradition and Daniélou's thesis that Clement's concept on Tradition derives its origin from the so-called Judeo-Christian literature of that period. Fortin finds in Clement's concept of Tradition Plato's philosophic tradition of antiquity. However, Fortin rightly believes that Clement did not accept two distinct and parallel traditions, one handed down by word of mouth from teacher to student and known only to a small elite within the Church, and another contained in writings that are the property of all. Cf. p. 43. It is worthy to note that Clement emphasizes the fact that unwritten teaching is revealed "through writing." *Stromata* 1, 1.

[74]*The Protocatechesis*, ch. 12 (and 17), ed. Frank L. Cross (London, 1960), pp. 7, 17, 47, 51.

[75]Ch. 1, 20.

[76]For the Greek text cf. *Ἡ Παράδοσις καὶ αἱ παραδόσεις*, in *Theologia* 34 (1963) 42-57.

[77]Chrysostomos Constantinides, *Ἡ σημασία τῆς Ἀνατολικῆς καὶ Δυτικῆς Παραδόσεως ἐν τῷ Χριστιανισμῷ*, in *Orthodoxia*, 35 (1960) 60 ff.

[78]*Letter to Pope Nicholas I*, ed. John Valettas (London, 1864), p. 157.

[79]Second Letter to the Non-Jurors. See in John Karmires, *Τὰ Δογματικὰ καὶ Συμβολικὰ Μνημεῖα τῆς Ὀρθοδόξου Καθολικῆς Ἐκκλησίας*, second edition (Athens, 1968), p. 899.

[80]Eusebios, E. H. 5, 24.

[81]*Adversus Haereses*, 1, 10. Cf. *Early Christian Fathers*, Vol. 1, p. 360.

[82]Ibid. 3, Preface. Cf. *Early Christian Fathers*, Vol. 1, p. 369.

[83]Ibid. 3, 2. Cf. *Early Christian Fathers*, Vol. 1, p. 371.

[84]Ibid. 3, 3. Cf. *Early Christian Fathers*, Vol. 1, pp. 371-72.

[85]Ibid. 3, 3. Cf. *Early Christian Fathers*, Vol. 1, p. 373.

[86]*Adversus Haereses*, 4, 26. See text in Quasten, *Patrology*, 1, 301.

[87]Eusebios, E. H., 5, 20.

[88]Florovsky, p. 185.

[89]*Adversus Haereses*, 3, 1. Cf. *Early Christian Fathers*, Vol. 1, p. 370.

[90]*De Praescriptione Haereticorum*, 20, 21.

[91]*First Letter to Serapion*, 28.

[92]""Ὥστε καὶ τὴν Παράδοσιν τῆς Ἐκκλησίας ἀξιόπιστον ἡγούμεθα· Παράδοσίς ἐστι μηδὲν πλέον ζήτει." *Ὁμιλία εἰς τὴν Β.' πρὸς Θεσσαλονικεῖς ἐπιστολήν*, PG 62.488; cf. also, col. 494.

[93]*Exposition of the Orthodox Faith*, Book 4, ch. 10. PG 94.1128; cf. *The Nicene and Post-Nicene Fathers*, 9, p. 79.

[94]PG 96.748.

[95]5.9.

28 The Mind of the Fathers

[96]Saint Basil, *Letter No. 92*.

[97]Cf. in H. Alivizatos, Οἱ Ἱεροὶ κανόνες, 2nd ed. (Athens, 1949), p. 187.

[98]PL 63.520B.

[99]Alexander Schmemann, "The Orthodox Tradition," in *The Convergence of Traditions*, ed. E. O'Brien (New York, 1967), p. 17.

[100]*On the Martyrdom of St. Polycarp*, ch. 12. In Lightfoot, p. 113.

[101]Robert M. Grant, "The Appeal to the Early Fathers," *Journal of Theological Studies*, 11 (1960) 13 ff.

[102]PG 25.225A and 26.688B.

[103]Ibid. 32.588B

[104]Collectio Conciliorum, 4, col 1184 ff.

[105]*Church History*, 34 (1965) 123 ff.

[106]Mansi, 4, 1184 ff.

[107]Nestorios, *The Bazaar of Heracleidis*, translated from the Syriac into English by G. R. Driver and L. Hodgson (Oxford, 1925), pp. 169, 173-74, 288, 245, 255, 378. Cf. also pp. 154, 168, 232, 236, 241-43. See also pp. 141 ff. where once more he appeals to the Fathers of the First Ecumenical Council of Nicea (325). He also appeals to Saint Athanasios (pp. 192, 200-02, 205-06, 221, 227, 236, 256, 261-62, 333); to Gregory the Theologian (pp. 200-02, 206, 220-21, 223-24, 227-28, 231, 245, 261). He appeals to Gregory of Nyssa (p. 221), to Saint Basil the Great (pp. 332-33). Of course, he claims that Diodoros of Tarsus and Theodore of Mopsuestia are "common Fathers of all" since Saint Basil the Great and Gregory the Theologian never condemned them, but that it is natural since they were his spiritual teachers and fathers. Cf. also his references to Saint Ambrose (pp. 191, 224, 229, 236, 256, 261). There is no doubt that the concept of Patristic Tradition in Nestorios is more narrow and limited than that of Cyril's, that is he does not appeal to all the Fathers as Cyril does, but rather he appeals to the Fathers of the Council of Nicaea (325), but although his concept of patristic tradition is somewhat weak, still however we cannot claim that he completely ignored the Fathers of the Church and neglected the non-Antiochene Fathers. See my book on Nestorios, *Contributions to the Studies of Nestorios*, in Greek (Athens, 1964), pp. 168 ff.

[108]Ibid. p. 201 ff

[109]Wilken, p. 141.

[110]Saint Basil makes it clear that the Church must "proclaim the faith of the Fathers, without any evasion," Letter 92. Did really Nestorios understand this in its full meaning? We doubt.

[111]James Moffatt, *The Thrill of Tradition* (New York, 1944).

[112]*On the Holy Spirit*, ch. 15. *The Nicene and the Post-Nicene Fathers*, 8, p. 22.

[113]John Karmires, Τὰ Δογματικὰ καὶ Συμβολικὰ Μνημεῖα τῆς Ὀρθοδόξου Καθολικῆς Ἐκκλησίας (Athens, 1960), p. 175. Cf. also, *Nicene and Post-Nicene Fathers*, ed. P. Schaff and H. Wage (Grand Rapids, 1956), 14, p. 264. See also J. H. Crehan, "Patristic Evidence for the Inspiration of Councils," *Studia Patristica*, Vol. 9, p. 210 ff.

[114]Georges Florovsky, "Saint Gregory Palamas and the Tradition of the

Fathers," in *The Greek Orthodox Theological Review*, 5 (1960) 120.

[115]Eusebios, E. H. 5, 28.

[116]*Contra Arian.*, 1, 40.

[117]*Contra Epist. Fundamenti*, 5, 6.

[118]Enarr. in Ps. 127 and 121.5.

[119]PG 90.120C.

[120]The first quotation is taken from the *Apostolic Constitutions*, Book 7, 41. The second quotation comes from the *Reply of the Eastern Patriarchs to Pope Pius IX in 1848*. Cf. Karmires, vol. 2, p. 920. The Greek text is as follows: "... διότι ὁ ὑπερασπιστὴς τῆς θρησκείας ἐστὶν αὐτὸ τὸ σῶμα τῆς Ἐκκλησίας, ἤτοι αὐτὸς ὁ λαός, ὅστις ἐθέλει τὸ θρήσκευμα αὐτοῦ αἰωνίως ἀμετάβλητον καὶ ὁμοειδὲς τῷ τῶν Πατέρων ..." Cf. also the article of T. J. Towers, "The Value of the Fathers," in *The Church Quarterly Review* (July-Sept., 1965), p. 299.

[121]*Commonitorium*, cap. 2, 3.

[122]Ὁδηγὸς H., PG 89.121. Cf. Markos Siotis, *Die Ekklesiologie als Grundlage der Neutestamentlichen Auslegung in der Grieschischen Orthodoxen Kirche* (Athens, 1960), p. 5, n. 2. Sonderabdruck aus der *Theologia*, Bd. 31, Hft. 4. Cf. also George S. Bebis, *Contributions to the Studies of Nestorios*, in Greek (Athens, 1964), p. 116.

[123]Pan. Christou, Ὁ Ὑπαρκτικὸς κατὰ τοὺς θεολόγους τῆς Καππαδοκίας (Thessalonike, 1961). That the Fathers were interested not only in abstract theological discussions but in reality that they cared for man, has been shown in a brilliant way by Fr. D. J. Constantelos in his already celebrated book *Byzantine Philanthropy and Social Welfare*, Rutgers Byzantine Series (New Brunswick, N.J., 1968).

[124]Neilos, *Letters*, 3, 27, 3, 84, 4, 59, 3,33.

[125]Neilos, *Letters*, 2, 66, 3, 33.

[126]Symeon the New Theologian, Λόγος Ἑξηκοστός, ed. and trans. Διονυσίου Ζαγοραίου (Athens), p. 316.

[127]Gregory Palamas, Ὑπὲρ Ἡσυχαζόντων, 1, 3, 42. Cf. Pan. Christou, Γρηγορίου Παλαμᾶ Συγγράμματα (Thessalonike, 1962), 2, p. 53.

[128]*De Vita Moysis*, ed. W. Jaeger and H. Musurillo (Leiden, 1964), pp. 112, 113, 116, 118, 43, 86, 82, 142, 139, 97, 83, 114. Cf. also George S. Bebis, "Gregory of Nyssa's 'De Vita Moysis': A Philosophical and Theological Analysis," *The Greek Orthodox Theological Review*, 12 (1967) 381, 388, 389, 390-91, 392.

Worship in the Orthodox Church

Introduction

Worship is widely defined and described as an act of honor, dignity, reverence, homage, and veneration for a deity. For us Christians (and especially for Orthodox Christians), worship has a more profound meaning. It signifies a continuous and an increasing experience which is nothing less than a real communion with our God, the Father Almighty, the Creator of all things visible and invisible; a participation in the life of Jesus Christ, whose life is extended and thrives in the Church; and the unending reception of the Holy Spirit, who strengthens our life and prepares us to become members of the divine and heavenly household of God.

In the confusion and turmoil of our modern world where life is lived frantically in pursuit of pleasure and good times, people find it hard to understand the supreme pleasure and real joy they can derive from the life of the Church, which is primarily a life of worship and prayer.

What is worship really? Is it relevant to our contemporary needs and aspirations? What are its goals and purposes, its means and methods? Is worship really helpful today, when technology has penetrated all the limits of imagination and when the first Russian cosmonaut sarcastically claimed that he saw no God in the skies while he was cruising in his spacecraft?

God of course exists, for although history, science, and psychology cannot pinpoint him, human experience feels his presence, and God himself revealed his existence and presence in history and in the life of mankind. Indeed, this is the ultimate purpose of worship, to bring man closer to God: to make our communion with him a living reality and to transform our lives into vessels of glory and blessing. This can be found only in the life of the Church.

30

The Definition of Worship: Its Task and Purpose

Worship is not mainly an act of the intellect. It is rather an experience in which the totality of the human existence participates and enjoys. Therefore, it is hard or even impossible to give a full technical definition. Indeed, attempts have been made to define, or at least to explain, worship. For instance, worship has been described as a response of the creature to the Eternal; or as an act through which a personal being addresses another personal being, superior and divine, that is God; or as a dialogue between God and man, or as the peculiar practical proof of religion, as a fundamental element of genuine piety. All these definitions are correct but something is still lacking. Man cannot fully explain or define something which in its roots is divine and has a divine purpose.

Actually, worship is a gift given by God to man. We read in the Book of Genesis that "God created man in the image of himself, in the image of God he created him, male and female he created them . . ." (Gen 1.27). When we read that God said, "Let us make man in our own image, in likeness of ourselves" (Gen 1.26), we can see here the gift of "communion," the immediate relationship, the proximity, the confidence which is offered to man, together with the gift of longing and desire to come closer and closer to God and become 'god.' Moses, the great prophet and liberator of the people of Israel whom God "knew face to face," knew how to use this gift of worship. For this reason he asked God on Mount Sinai, "Show me your glory, I beg you . . ." (Ex 33.18), and when God kept his promise and let all his splendor pass in front of him and pronounced his name before him, then Moses "bowed down to the ground at once and worshipped." "If I have, indeed, won your favor, Lord," he said, "let my Lord come with us, I beg . . ." (Ex 34.20). This is probably the most ancient and complete account of worship in the Old Testament. Later, the prophets of Israel — Amos, Hosea, Micah, Isaiah, and Jeremiah — set an example of pure, moral, and filial worship.

To be sure, worship is not all a Jewish or Christian phenomenon. The Indians, the Babylonians, the Egyptians, the peoples of the Americas, and the ancient Greeks and Romans all worshiped, prayed, and offered respect to their deities. However, their worship is mostly materialistic, mechanical, magical, or many times is full of mythological and magical speculation, pale abstract fantasies or cold rationalistic techniques and formulas.

Christian worship takes place on a personal level. Man as a wholesome and full personality communicates with God, who is not an abstract, illogical deity, but the Holy Trinity: the persons of the Father, of the Son, and of the Holy Spirit. There is a passionate yearning, a humble surrender, a gentle and quiet intimacy, a rapturous and unspeakable delight and joy in Christian worship. The relationship of Father to Son can be visualized; the absolute love of man for God and God's love for man, the unfathomable revelation of God's will in the hearts of his people, all these make Christian worship a distinct, powerful, and harmonious way of life. It is an experience which cannot be described in human terms and categories. As such, Christian worship is self-consuming; it is an unending fire in the souls of people, an intensified and ineffable mystery in the life of God's blessedness and bliss, and a continuous movement and inner struggle to reach union with God. This may sound paradoxical, especially in the context of contemporary popular parlance, where sometimes worship appears as an individualistic expression of one's own self who likes "to do his own thing," regardless of what the Church teaches and what our Lord commanded us to do. It is our choice to make a commitment to our Lord Jesus Christ or to the expediences of this world.

Saint Paul, the greatest missionary apostle of the early Church, describes the Christian way of life as nothing less than a life of worship which is a "spiritual revolution . . . so that you can put on the new self that has been created in God's way, in the goodness and holiness of the truth" (Eph 4.23). Paul admonishes the people of the church in Ephesos again, saying, "Try, then, to imitate God, as children of his that he loves, and follow Christ by loving as he loved you, giving himself up in our place as a fragrant offering and a sacrifice to God" (Eph 5.1-2). He advises his people to "sing the words and tunes of the psalms and hymns when you are together, and go on singing and chanting to the Lord in your hearts, so that always and everywhere you are giving thanks to God who is our Father in the name of our Lord Jesus Christ" (Eph 5.19-20).

In defining the meaning of worship more concretely, Saint Paul writes to the Church of Rome,

> O the depth of the riches and wisdom and knowledge of God! How unsearchable are his judgments and how inscrutable his ways! For who has known the mind of the Lord, or who has been his counselor? Or who has given a gift to him that he might be repaid? For from him and through him and to him are all things. To him be be glory for ever . . . I appeal to you therefore, brethren, by the mercies of God, to present your bodies as a living sacrifice, holy and acceptable to God, which is your spiritual worship. Do not be conformed to this world but be transformed by the renewal of your mind, that you may prove what is the will of God, what is good and acceptable and perfect . . . (Rom 11.33-36; 12.1-2).

Here we have a clear description of the essence of Christian worship. For Saint Paul, worship is a "spiritual revolution" (*ananeosis* in Greek), a continuous renewal which transforms life to "a sweet-smelling savor," or to a life of sacrifice (as was Christ's life), a life of goodness and holiness and truth. Worship is a singing of hymns, which springs out of the hearts of men; a spontaneous thanksgiving for all God's gifts in life; a remodeling of our behavior according to the will of God, which pleases God and makes our existence as rational and intelligent beings worthy of God. When we say intelligent or rational beings, we do not simply mean people who have studied the knowledge offered in our schools, but as Saint Anthony, the great monk of the fourth century says, "A truly intelligent man has only one care — whole-heartedly to obey Almighty God and to please him. The one and only thing he teaches his soul is how best to do things agreeable to God, thanking him for his merciful providence in whatever may happen in his life. . . . In this understanding and this faith in God lie salvation and peace of soul."

Peace of soul is a very important element in Christian worship. Only by worshiping God can we secure for ourselves peace of soul. Because as Saint Basil, the famous bishop of Caesarea, writes, "One cannot approach the knowledge of the truth with a disturbed heart." Only through worship can man obtain an inner feeling of security and peace. Through absolute trust and unreserved confidence in God the Father, man receives the response of fatherly love, guidance, and direction needed in life. Man becomes free and liberated from the burden of emotional and physical barriers and is ready to enjoy the life of spiritual uplifting, which is nothing less than to communicate with the glory and the happy radiance of his Creator. This is why Christ said if he who is the Son of God makes us free, we will be free indeed (Jn 8.36). Saint Paul admonishes us, saying, "When Christ freed us, he meant us to remain free. Stand firm, therefore, and do not submit to the yoke of slavery" (Gal 5.1).

But to feel this peace of soul and this freedom and liberation which every human being desires, one basic prerequisite is needed. This is humility. One must approach worship not as the pharisee of the Gospel who boasted and exalted himself as a man of virtue and perfection, but he must approach the altar of God as the tax collector, who surrenders his whole being under the mercy of God and who utters, "God be merciful to me, a sinner" (Lk 18.9-14). Indeed, to be humble is not an easy thing. One must renounce his previous way of life; he must forget the pleasures of our contemporary society, and he must renounce his ego and its selfish pursuits and goals. A proud man cannot become a man of prayer. For he cannot accept his sinfulness and shortcomings, and, more important, he cannot acknowledge his total dependence on God, who is creator and provider.

Another prerequisite for true worship is cleanliness and purity, for it is through this that we must approach and communicate with God. We are all sinners; nobody is perfect in this world. Temptations in life are manifold and can appear even at the most sacred moments of prayer and meditation. This is why in the eucharistic prayer we ask the Lord, "Cleanse the thoughts of our hearts by the inspiration of the Holy Spirit, that we may perfectly love you and worthily magnify your Holy Name." Again in the second prayer for the faithful in the Liturgy we pray, "Purify our souls and bodies from all carnal and spiritual defilement, and grant that our presence at your holy altar may be innocent and blameless..."

How can this purity become a reality in the lives of the people of today? Purity of heart is not an immovable and static state of life. It is something we must strive for during our whole life. It is a mountain we must often climb during our journey in this world. We may stop or fall back at times during this ascent, but we should continue to climb and ascend towards purity, that purity which will liberate us from the demands of our own self and of our environment. It is not an easy task. But the reward of liberation is worthy of trying to reach that stage, when the goal of both body and soul is to express our faith and love to God the Father, to families, friends, and to all fellowmen.

Some people make a distinction between worship and prayer. Worship is "essentially disinterested" with human realities and "means only God," whereas prayer seeks to satisfy the inner yearnings and urgencies of the human soul. Worship means adoration; prayer signifies needs and involvement in the current problems of contemporary life. But this distinction is rather external and superficial. The fact is that worship is the total surrender of our own self to God. Adoration and petition, praise and intercession, thanksgiving and asking for something overlap and intermingle. Of course, there is no doubt that worship is expressed through some kind of ritual. Ceremonies, music and sound, verbal formulas, even "theatrical" movements and gestures are parts and elements of these rituals. Ritual stimulates the human heart and body to express their feelings of devotion. It provokes a psychological setting for both the individual and corporate acts of worship. Ritual develops the feeling of participation in the divine life, in the acts of God which are manifested in his creatures and in the act of salvation fulfilled by Jesus Christ on the cross. Actually, all of time and space is brought into the framework of Christian worship. Thus does Saint Paul write, "From the beginning till now the entire creation, as we know, has been groaning in one great act of giving birth; and not only creation but all of us who possess the first fruits of the Spirit, we too groan inwardly as we wait for our bodies to be set free . . .'' (Rom 8.22-23).

Ritual, however elaborate, cannot unite us with God unless it takes place in the Spirit of God, that is, in the true spirit of self-dedication to the Holy Trinity. Our Lord himself made this clear when he proclaimed that "God is Spirit, and they that worship him must worship him in Spirit and in truth" (Jn 4.24). Nothing can or must separate us from the real union with God. As Saint Paul so characteristically wrote, "I am certain of this: neither death not life, no angel, nor prince, nothing that exists, nothing still to come, not any power, or height or depth, nor any created thing, can ever come between us and the love of God made visible in Christ Jesus our Lord" (Rom 8.38-39).

Still one might ask: What is really the definition, the meaning and the task of worship? We might rightly say that worship is the style of life which is occupied with unceasing prayer (1 Thes 5.17); or the act of the Chistian who " . . . at all times preserves the memory of God . . . in order that he may show love to the Lord not only when he goes into the place of prayer, but also when he is walking, talking, or eating, that he may preserve the memory of God and a sense of love and yearning toward him"[1] Writes Saint Basil, "Prayer is a request for what is good, offered by the devout to God. But we do not restrict the 'request' simply to what is stated in words . . . we should not express our prayer merely in syllables, but the power of prayer should be expressed in the moral attitude of our soul and in the virtuous actions that extend through our life . . . This is how you pray continually — not by offering prayer in words, but by joining yourself to God through your whole way of life, so that your life becomes one continuous and uninterrupted prayer . . ."[2]

The Main Characteristics of Our Worship

We have spoken about individual, personal or private worship, and about public or corporate worship. Both are indispensable. We must enter our own private rooms and in front of holy icons search ourselves. We must not permit our mind to be scattered here and there, but in self-discipline and self-control we ought to open the depths of our heart and pour out feelings of adoration, thanksgiving, praise, devotion, and dedication, as well as our request and petitions. In the morning and in the evening we will recite the Lord's Prayer, and read from service books and other devotional literature of the Church.

So far so good. But this is not enough. Christian worship finds its fulfillment in the form of corporate worship. Corporate worship means our participation in the common worship of the Church, our frequent presence in the services sung in our churches, our active fellowship in the temple of God, and our constant, participation in the sacraments or mysteries of the Holy Church.

Many people today question the value of going to church. We could pray at home so why should we go to church? This is the weakest argument, and the most superficial pretext to avoid the Church. To be sure, the Church never asks her children to come to the church merely out of habit or out of an unhealthy fanaticism or militancy. The Church, however, makes clear to her faithful that "you cannot have God as your father unless you have the Church as your mother," to use the famous expression of Saint Cyprian. The Church, as a good and affectionate mother, cares and nourishes her children with spiritual food and provides all the means for the spiritual welfare of her people. Moreover, the Church, being the very body of Christ, requires her people to participate and live her life so that all her faithful become members of the body of Christ and "heirs of God and co-heirs with Christ, sharing his sufferings so as to share his glory" (Rom 8. 17).

We must remember at the same time that Christian worship has two dimensions — the vertical and the horizontal. The vertical dimension brings us to direct contact and union with God. The horizontal dimension brings us to a true fellowship with our brothers and sisters in Christ, who gather together in the Church for common worship to a common Father, the Creator of all things: to Jesus Christ, who brought us the good tidings of salvation; and to the Holy Spirit, who abides with and strengthens the Church. We may paraphrase a well-known dictum and say that those who pray together, stay together. It is interesting to note that throughout our Divine Liturgy the plural *we* and *us* are used extensively. "Again, we pray . . ." is repeatedly found in the Liturgy. "Let us love one another . . ." the priest proclaims to the congregation. The ancient Latin Christians realized the great significance or corporate worship when they would utter, *unus Christianus, nullus Christianus*, which means that one Christian is not being a Christian at all: "One cannot divide Christ . . .," Saint Cyril of Alexandria states in a most vigorous and convincing way.[3] He is absolutely right, because in the Church all teh people of God, who are the fullness of the body of Christ, gather and worship in the name of Christ and in full communion with the Holy Spirit. Only in the Church the concord of faith exists, where the bread of heaven and the cup of salvation sanctify the soul and body of man.[4] Only in the Church can Christians become a true "Communion of saints." Saint Paul writes, "We are one body in Christ" (Rom 12.5), and this oneness is fulfilled in the Church. Only in the Church is there salvation. A famous Russian theologian used to say, "We know that when any one of us falls, he falls alone; but no one is saved alone. He is saved in the Church, as a member of her, and in union with all her other members." Or to put it in another way, "There is no other way to be saved except through our neighbor." Both clergy and laity, the living and the departed, the Virgin Mary and the Fathers of the Church and the martyrs, all these are members of the "communion of saints" with whom we are united through the bond of love and faith and hope.

To pray alone at home is commendable. But this is not enough. Only in the common gathering of the people of God and fullness of our salvation can union with the Divine become a reality and transform our life into an experience of personal encounter with God.

This encounter with God makes our worship theocentric. The whole circle of the liturgical services of the Church moves around God, who is incomprehensible by nature and whom no human reason or human tongue can describe. The fact that all the human services of the Church begin with a doxology to the Holy Trinity (Blessed is the kingdom of the Father, and of the Son, and of the Holy Spirit"), shows that our worship turns its attention towards the personal God, who was revealed in the Scriptures, who sent his only begotten Son to liberate us from the bondage of sin, and who sends the Holy Spirit to breathe life into the Church. Thus, we may also say that our worship is christological and pneumatological. Christological because the Church is herself the very body of Christ and because the entire liturgical year is in reality a reenactment of the Lord's life on the earth. The Annunciation, the birth of Christ from the Holy Virgin, the baptism in the river Jordan, his death and resurrection, his ascension and his transfiguration are main events which are celebrated throughout the year by the Church in a most festive way. The Divine Liturgy, with the eucharist as its center, is nothing less than a step by step enactment of Christ's life, his preaching, his sufferings, his sacrifice on the Cross, and his glorious resurrection.

Our worship is also catholic and ecumenical in the sense that it ignores geographical boundaries, racial prejudices, language barriers, and national distinctions. The *Didache*, a small book written at the end of the first century A. D. by an unknown author, presents a picturesque description of this reality when the priest prays, saying, "As this broken bread was scattered over hills and then, when gathered became one, so may the Church be gathered from the ends of the earth into Thy kingdom." In the Liturgy of Saint Basil the priest prays, "Have in remembrance also, O Lord, we beseech Thee, the Holy catholic and apostolic

Church, which is from all ends of the universe . . ."

Our worship is also eschatological (from the Greek word *eschaton* the end), which means that in our worship we are anticipating the world to come and we taste of the fruits of the glorious joy of the everlasting life. Death, resurrection, and judgment, our last encounter with God in front of the throne of his eternal glory, all are integral parts of our worship. Here the anticipation of the sweetness of seeing God is mentioned, and faith and hope in the righteous judgment of God is proclaimed.

We must mention here too, that our worship is biblical and is based on the pure origins of the liturgical experience of the early Church. When we say that our worship is biblical, we mean that it has its historicl roots in the Bible and that in every service it includes readings from the Old and the New Testament. As far as its early and ancient basis, a noted Orthodox scholar wrote not long ago, "The Orthodox Church has preserved the liturgical spirit of the early Church and continues to live by it and to be nourished from it as from her purest source . . ."

Finally, our worship is mystical, not in a magical sense, but in a mysterious way which is hidden and unexplainable. There is an unceasing uplifting of the heart, which cannot be explained in human words. There is a secret dialogue between Creator and creture, which culminates in the union of man with God in the Liturgy. The redemptive power of Christ is working in an unspoken way in the heart of the believer, and the Holy Spirit is operating and directing the human soul towards its perfection and salvation. How do these things happen? No one knows. Saint Augustine replied, "The Church said it. Ask no more . . . "

How can this admonition be reconciled with the curiosity and the rationalistic spirit which prevails in our contemporary world? Everyone wants to know why, where, and how things happened. This is a legitimate claim, and the Church must still answer all the questions people submit to her. However, the Church reminds us that she speaks not only for pragmatic and empirical things. The Church herself is 'theanthropic,' that is, she is both divine and human, as Christ was both God and man. The presence of the Church in this world is a witness of this truth — " . . . our knowledge is imperfect and our prophesying is imperfect; but once perfection comes, all imperfect things will disappear . . . Now we are seeing a dim reflecton in a mirror, but then we shall be seeing face to face. The knowledge that I have now is imperfect; but then I shall know as fully as I am known" (1 Cor 13.9-12). If everything was already known to us worship would lose much of its meaning. God that is needed for our salvation and He gave us the foretaste of the final transfiguration in which "God shall be all in all" and nothing will be hidden.

The Church, therefore, as a cosmic or as a human reality, offers us all the means necessary to partake in the mystery of salvation and to transform us from this life into members of Christ's body and participants in the kingdom of God, which will follow after this life on earth. These means, to be sure, are not merely empirical means. They are both divine and human, combining both the earthly exoteric appearance of created things and the inner esoteric blessing of the unseen energies of God.

What are these means and ways of worship? Individual and corporate prayer is one of the many means of worship, and we have already spoken about these. We also have spoken about ritual in which people find ways of expressing their inner feelings with verbal formulas and physical movements. But the way and means of worship are various. The church, as the temple of God, which is divided into the nave and sanctuary of the altar, is an excellent way of expressing the reality of both the heavenly and the earthly kingdom of God where the Holy Trinity and all the saints, the living and the departed, comprise the mystical communion of the divine and human. The icons are especially significant, from both the aesthetic and theological points of view, because in the form of painting they present the triumphant Church of Christ. We do not adore the icons. Adoration is to be given only to God. But we honor the holy persons they depict. Through this, the Church militant, those members of the Church who are still living, come into close communion with the Church triumphant. The vestments of the clergy, which carry a profound symbolic meaning, the incense, the bells, the singing, even our alms to the Church are ways and means through which we express our respect, our gratitude, debt, adoration, and honor to our Creator. Not that God needs them, because God is above and beyond any need. But all these ways and means are for our own edification, spiritual advancement, and inner gratification.

Preaching is one of the most important methods of showing a true spirit of worship. Both the preacher and the hearer derive from the Bible and traditions of the Church the same source of wisdom. Therefore, both have a panoramic view of God's action in history. The spoken word of God is as refreshing water in the thirsty souls of men and leads them onto the road of repentance, rehabilitation, and spiritual renewal in the Church of Christ.

And what about the sacraments of the Church? The precise wording for this in our Church is the mysteries (*mysteria*). The Church uses this term because as Saint John Chrysostom so pertinently wrote, ". . .what we believe is not what we see, but we see one thing and believe another . . . (*Homily on 1 Cor.* 5.1; PG 61.55).

The Church accepts seven sacraments of mysteries — (1) baptism, (2) chrismation or chrism, (3) the eucharist, (4) repentance or confesson, (5) holy order of ordination, (6) marriage, and (7) holy unction. All the mysteries belong to the sphere of one great mystery, salvation and redemption through Jesus Christ, which actually was "the message which was a mystery hidden for generations and centuries and has now been revealed to his saints . . . The mystery is Christ among you . . ." (Col 1.26-17).

The breaking of the communion with God through the transgression of man brought the fall of man and creation into death and corruption. Through baptism we come to a new life, to the new community of the people of God. The remission of sins is given to the baptized and the neophyte is saved and regenerated and becomes a true and genuine member of the Church. Through chrismation, the seal of the Holy Spirit, the body of the newly-baptized is anointed as a positive sign that man has been adopted by God and that the Holy Spirit dwells in the soul of the neophyte, who is ready to receive holy communion.

Now if by baptism and chrismation we become related with God and with one another by "adoption," through the eucharist this relation becomes one of blood. "We came in communion in Christ and with (his) passion and divinity" Saint Gregory the Theologian, *Oration*, 4:52). Saint Ignatios of Antioch noted that the eucharist becomes the medicine of immortality and the antidote so that we should not die but live forever in Jesus Christ.

Through the sacrament or the mystery of confession or penance we are restored again in the position of liberation from the burden of sins committed after our baptism. Contemporary psychology confirms the valuable contribution of confession and penance to the stabiltiy of the human personality.

Through the mystery of ordination the grace of God sets apart, but not as intermediaries between God and man, the special duties of the clergy to preserve the charismatic and sacramental life of the Church and to preserve the Christian community through the sacraments, preaching, and an exemplary way of life which resists the temptations of life and the evils of divisions — immortality and apostasy.

The mystery of marriage unites two souls and two bodies in the unity of love and understanding. The deep meaning in the mystery of marriage prompted Saint Paul to liken and compare that union with the mystery of the union between Christ and his Church: ". . . since as Christ is head of the Church and saves the whole body, as is a husband the head of his wife; and as the Church submits to Christ, so should wives to their husbands, in everything. Husbands should love their wives just as Christ loved the Church and sacrificed himself for her to make her holy . . ." (Eph 5.21-33).

Holy unction offers consolation and healing to the mentally and physically ill. Through the holy and blessed oil the priest and the believer receive the power of the Holy Spirit, which brings peace of soul and spiritual healing upon the wounds which beset all men because of the vicissitude of life.

Thus, we have seen that the Church uses all the means which Christ gave her for the presentation of our faith, for perseverance of our faith, and for our restoration to kingdom of God. This is a process which begins during our life on earth and is continued eternally in life everlasting.

Worship and Modern Man

Many people question the practical value and the spiritual meaning of our worship. They think that sermons are a "drag," that the services are completely irrelevant, and that the Church cannot respond to the needs of contemporary technological society. As one American scholar noted not long ago, with a cold sense of sarcasm, the new priests of to-day are the mathematicians, the people in the laboratory, the technologists.

Many people look for change. But change into what? Many churches in America have proceeded through deep and lasting changes. Even the Roman Catholic Church introduced new forms of liturgy, which were not new in essence, but were innovations based on the practice of the early Church. Modern musical instruments, modern methods of singing, even dances have been introduced to many liturgical traditions in America. What about the Orthodox Church? Now, one must take special note that these changes did not practically attract many people to the Gospel and the Church.

The Church, naturally, is not static. Its liturgical forms and norms are in a constant process of development and change. We who live in this country do not realize that our church life has been influenced by American mannerisms. The hour of the services, the fasting rules, the organ, the presence of priests without beards, the building of edifices to facilitate schooling, athletics, and social gatherings, are some of the changes imposed on the life of the Church in this society.

But we must realize that although the external character of liturgy may change (change in the use of languages to adapt to the worship needs of our faithful), the essence of the Church never changes. The essence of our worship cannot change. We may lower our 'iconostasion' (the icon screen which divides the sanctuary from the nave as it used to be in the early times of our Church); we may translate and use the vernacular languages in our services; we may even consider rewriting services or experimenting with new forms of worship. But the mystery which is Christ himself will never change. "Jesus Christ is the same today as he was yesterday and as he will be for ever" (Heb 13.8).

The great mystery of the Church will always center on Christ, and the eucharistic offering of the Church will always be the same in essence because Christ founded his church and his eucharist as means of salvation, reconciliation and communion with God.

We cannot, and we should not, expect an established paradise on earth. Happiness is not to be found, in its absolute form, in this life. Only in the spirit of true worship, where the barriers of the world and its demands fall apart, only there can we find the fullness and the wholesomeness of life. Worship must become a way of life, an experience which need not change, a fulfillment and full restoration in the love of God and in the love of our fellowmen. Finally, worship is an act of love, and love can never change. It remains always burning in the hearts of the faithful, increasing, developing, but in essence always remaining the same. This is the message of salvation and the calling to a real union between God and man.

Eusebios and His Theology of History

The title of this work may seem at the outset very strange indeed. Modern thinkers, philosophers, and theologians as well use mostly the term "philosophy of history," which term applies to theological treatises such as Augustine's "Civitate Dei." Georges Florovsky has already objected to the use of this terminology for the simple reason that in the Church Fathers especially, the basic notion which underlies their works is God himself, from whom all things come and to whom all things are led. In fact, Professor Florovsky rightly asserts that all modern "philosophies of history" have been crypto-theological, or probably pseudo-theological. More especially, for the Christian historian, history becomes "the history of salvation," *die Heilsgeschichte*, whose beginning, center, and end coincide in the person of the Redeemer.[1] G. La Piana has rightly observed that:

> . . . the term "philosophy of history" as applied to this and similar methods of historical interpretation is altogether misleading. More properly, this type of philosophy of history is a theology of history, inasmuch as its fundamental premises, on which the whole structure is built and stands, come from religious beliefs and from their theological elaborations about the nature of the universe, of man and his destiny. History written from this point of view becomes apologetics. The method of history suggested or imposed by theological premises cannot be other than a theological method. It remains fundamentally a theological method even when the historians who follow it use the most refined instruments supplied by modern historical criticism in dealing with specific problems or aspects of history.[2]

43

La Piana's words are especially applicable to Eusebios. For indeed, Eusebios' approach to history is, we might say, theological in the pure sense of the word. This premise might lead the reader to another question. Can we really speak of theology of history in Eusebios' works? Is it not true that in reality Eusebios was just a chronographer, a copyist, a collector, as a matter of fact, of documents, and nothing more? It is true, of course, that Eusebios writes as an annalist. But beneath the chronological data and the strict and dry presentation of factual history lies the vision of a man who had already penetrated the very meaning of history as such. We may agree with Lightfoot that Eusebios' style is "especially vicious."[3] But nobody can deny that Eusebios' writings have touched the very soul of history, that is to say, the great plan which leads and directs history to a great purpose towards the fulfilment of the mystery of salvation and the accomplishment of the redemption of man.[4]

Eusebios was born about the year 263. He was born probably in Palestine and was educated in Antioch and Caesarea in Palestine, having thus the influence of both the Antiochian and the Alexandrian schools of thought.[5] He was very fortunate indeed to have had as his friend, guide, and supporter the pious and learned presbyter Pamphilos of Caesarea, who introduced Eusebios to the vast field of scientific research of biblical, patristic, Christian and non-Christian documents. Later, after the martyrdom of Pamphilos in 309 in the persecution under Diocletian, Eusebios, as a token of his love for his master and colleague, took the latter's name as his own surname. Eusebios did not himself escape the consequences of the persecutions and he was imprisoned, though he soon was released from this imprisonment.[6] About the year 315, or perhaps a little earlier, he was chosen bishop of Caesarea. He remained bishop of this great city until his death in 340. Although he did not identify himself with the Orthodox position in the Arian controversy, Eusebios' name figures even among saints and confessors in the so-called *Martyrologium Syriacum* (fifth century), where his memory is celebrated on May 30.

In the so-called *Martyrologium Hieronymianum*, Eusebios' name is entered under two different dates, March 5 and June 21. We do not know whether the compiler of the "Syriac Martyrology" was an Arian, or whether out of gratitude he inserted the name of Eusebios in the *Martyrologium*. Honigmann has discussed the problem without any conclusive solution.[7] In any case Severos of Antioch informs us that Cyril Alexandria on his way to Ephesos (for the Council of Ephesos, 431), visited

Caesarea and had Eusebios' name removed from the diptychs of the Church of Caesarea.[8]

The discussion whether Eusebios was an Arian or a semi-Arian still continues. Indeed his attitude in the Arian controversy gave rise to many speculations concerning his character and his whole personality as well his whole position in the newly triumphant religion.[9] He was a mild and calm man, preferring to take always the middle way. His moderation and amiability led him to follow a middle course in the Arian controversy and this shows that virtues such as moderation and amiability are not always good guidelines in confronting exreme problems. Simply stated, Eusebios did not achieve an understanding of the spirit of his time, a time which demanded straight and positive decisions. Nevertheless, though Eusebios did not penetrate into the inward meaning of the Arian controversy, none the less was he a child of his time. The man with the gentle soul, the aristocratic courtesy and the mild and moderate character, could not remain untouched by the unprecedented change in the flow and current of history. A whole empire was falling. It was this very empire which had tried with extreme violence to destroy and erase the new religion of Christ. But instead of the destruction of Christianity, the dissolution of the Roman Empire was taking place. Its vitality and power of cohesion were diminishing and the attempts of ephemeral emperors and princes could not stop the disruption and degeneration of the state. The persecutions against the Christians were the last desperate movements of the dying lion. Eusebios himself lived the heroic drama of the persecutions. Eusebios himself witnessed the sacrificial spirit and enthusiasm which inflamed and inspired immense number of martyrs. Further, he suffered imprisonment and saw the martyrdom of his great friend, protector and teacher, Pamphilos. Moreover, Christian worship, for centuries, had laid hidden behind the shut doors of secret places and the "Disciplina Arcani" had guided the whole of Christian life.

Suddenly, the bloodshed stopped. The shut doors of the catacombs opened. The contempt decreased. The religion of the poor Jew became a free religion. Yet only a free religion? Something more. Something really momentous. It became the religion of the emperor and gradually the religion of the state. Eusebios' joy and happiness is thoroughly justified. The miracle, i.e. the victory of Christianity fascinated him. Naturally, therefore, all his writings bear the feelings and admiration and astonishment in the unfolding process of history which, beyond any doubt, is developed under the strong hand of God. History reveals the great plan and purpose of God, and it is the area in which eternal truth has been confirmed. Eusebios' *Ecclesiastical History*, therefore, does not lie only in the sphere of chronography as some scholars supposed. Because, for Eusebios, the divergent historical facts were not just occurences for which a plain chronological arrangement would be sufficient for the human intellect. Not at all. For Eusebios, the divergent facts of history became obviously events with a profound meaning. Here, the theological interpretation of history comes to the surface. The numbers and the dates and the places become events with meaningful insight, with a mystical approach and rewarding curiosity. Apparently, all the events have for Eusebios their causes, their purpose. Their setting in the great framework of the divine providence was obvious to Eusebios. This notion underlies all the works of Eusebios and we shall have many opportunities later in this paper to experience his approach and insight.

It is true that if we define genius as having the qualification of originality, then we must confess, that Eusebios was not a genius and therefore original in his thoughts. But he was original in his intentions, as he decided, first to write down the history of the victorious Christian Church, a task for which he won the title of the Father of Church History, as well as the gratitude of the whole Church in the centuries that followed and in the centuries which will come.

We spoke already for Eusebios' inclination towards Origenism. Eusebios in fact was an Origenist.[10] Still it is quite difficult for historical criticism to decide to what extent Origen influenced Eusebios. But without a doubt we can detect the impact which the Alexandrian scholar left of Eusebios, if we detect the allegorical method and approach in Eusebios' writings which are beyond question. Besides, the world-scheme plan, i.e. the "economy," which characterizes so much of the theology of Origen is very apparent, as we have already said, in Eusebios' writings. Eusebios as a matter of fact was born in the cross-road of the empire where not only armies could meet but schools of thought and currents of scholarship as well. He was brought up in an atmosphere, where pagan, heretical a orthodox learning could intermingle. That he was influenced by all of them was natural. He inherited, first of all, the Thukydidean principles of precision, lacomicism and above all the principle that history should be necessarily a record of practical utility, i.e. history's primary goal should be the constructive teaching of its student.[11] Polybios,[12] Cicero and Tacitus considered history as a thing of use. Baur[13] has already noticed the parallelism between Herodotos and Eusebios, and Milburn[14] the parallelism between the latter and Josephus. Eusebios also follows the line of the two great Apologists, Justin the Martyr and Aristides. As a matter of fact, he surpasses them in many respects. He is more positive and logical, more precise a scholarly. Speaking of philosophy we quote Professor Lake, who rightly has observed that "part of his great claim to distinction is that when writings philosophy he never neglets history, or philosophy when writing history."[15] He lacks, of course, the profundity of the philosophical speculation and insight of Justin Martyr, Aristides, Clement of Alexandria and Origen. However, Eusebios outdoes all of them in the grasp of history, in presenting history in a clear-minded historical approach. Besides, Eusebios' erudition and tremendous learning classify him in the ranks of he most learned men of all epochs. He could embrace many-sided knowledge and arrange it in an admirable way. Lightfoot has observed, that he was an historian, apologist, topographer, exegete, critic, preacher and dogmatic writer.[16] Moreover, he was a productive writer and an indefatigable scholar, and collector of documentary material. He had the passion to discover and record facts, and to present them in their concise form. He was objective, impersonal and a relentless recorder of events. He was systematic in the course of his writings and careful, as far as he could, not become a victim of credulity or of distortion of the historical truth. His honesty and reliability cannot seriously be attacked. Of course, Eusebios had his own defects. He wrote in a rather dry literary fashion, and with a graceless style. His *Ecclesiastical History* especially presents that uncomfortable lack of easy continuity, which is especially felt in the biographies that many times are interrupted for the insertion of events. Many times also his scholarship is not analogous in depth as it in breadth and his judgment is not always critically sound. But his true historical instinct combined with scholastic accuracy and vast erudition make him a great historian — a historian whose theology of history would be extremely interesting for he modern scholar, since it was written by a man who witnessed the greatest moments of the victorious Christian Church.

The "*Chronikon*" or "*Chronicle*"[17] of Eusebios is indispensable for the student of his works because it presents in tables the course of history as Eusebios himself and the early Christians conceived it. As a matter of fact, this conception of history continues to prevail today among many modern Christian historians. To be sure, Eusebios perceived that the foundation of history is an accurate chronology upon which a conscientious historian should build and extend his historical scheme. Of course, chronology is dry and boring, but beneath the mathematical calculations is hidden a mysterious charm, the wonderful attraction of the hidden treasury under the frigid and insensitive veil of numbers. Shotwell[18] has already observed the great value of this *Chronikon*, in which "history is the reservoir not of argument but of proof, and the

proof is mathematical." But the most important thing here is that under
the mathematical table, Eusebios unfolds in front of our eyes a panoramic
description of history, a continuous, straightforward development of
events which are moving forward, always forward under the invisible eye
of God and according to his purposeful plan which underlines the whole
history. Eusebios is frank with himself and with his readers and from
the very beginning he informs them that no one should ever arrogantly
contend that a sure and a thorough knowledge of chronology is attainable.
On the contrary, everyone should remember the words of the Lord that
"It is not for you to know the times or the seasons, which the Father
has fixed by his own authority"(Acts 1.7).[19] With this introduction,
which shows the real sense of responsibility as well as the since sincere
feeling of humility which guided him in his works, Eusebios proceeds
with scientific and scholastic accuracy, remarkable for his day, in the
main part of his "Chronicle." From the point of view of theology of
history the most important points which must attract our attention are
the following. First of all, Eusebios believes in the universality and the
unity of history as such. Pagan, Jewish and Christian history are in reality
of one entity. They have one cause, one inward meaning, one purpose.
For Eusebios, history, world history, has one spring and fountain. The
divergent empires present the streams which came out in parallel lines
from creation and the original sin. They proceed in the course of history
in a straight line in order to reach their destination, which is, of course,
the new kingdom under Christ. As a matter of fact, God " . . . made
from one every nation of man to live on all the face of the earth"(Acts
17.26). This is one of the obvious lines of thought which underlies the
structure of the *Chronikon.* But the ultimate purpose of history, its
culmination, was the coming of Christ. Eusebios, practical as he is, hastens
to inform us of the prophecies which were made to Abraham and Daniel
for the coming of the Lord.[20] To be sure, this culmination of history was
not an end of history. Not at all. It was rather the starting point of a
new era, the Christian era, in which the Christian Church would carry
on the redemptive task of Christ in order to preach it in all the corners
of the earth. The coming of Christ was the beginning of a new epoch,
the epoch during which the Church would gather all peoples under one
Shepherd, in one flock, as he himself had predicted. (Jn 10.16). Another
important point, which the *Chronikon* of Eusebios emphasizes is of course
the conception of the continuity of history. Christianity is the legitimate
continuation of the Jewish religion, which Jewish religion was older than
the pagan cults. But if Christianity were the natural and physical con-

tinuation of the Jewish religion, nonetheless it was also the religion which should take the place of the pagan religions. The pagan religions were streams which should pour in the new basin in order to be substituted, by the new religion, the religion which by now started the new stream, the majestic the beautiful Christian current. To be sure, the whole fabric of the *Chronikon* is interwoven with an apologetic thread. It was an answer to those pagans and Jews who still recognized in Christianity an eccentric sect which without any prerogative was trying to establish itself in the course of world history. We shall have other opportunities to see in more expanded forms the thoughts of Eusebios concerning the theology of history. But we must always keep in mind that all these thoughts are based mostly on the *Chronography*. We may say that the general outline and the brief summary of Eusebios' works are found in his *Chronography*. And one more important point. The dates and the comments, and the details and the order of Eusebios' *Chronography* have played a tremendous role in the determination of the historical outlook of Europe, i.e. Europe's history was influenced, and the influence continues to exist, from that little book of Eusebios. As a matter of fact the whole history of the world owes to Eusebios its general form and frame.

This is not the place to discuss the date, the occasion and the circumstances under which Eusebios' *Preparation for the Gospels* was written.[21] But we must point out from the very beginning that Eusebios' main goal was to prove that all the events which preceded the foundation of the Christian Church and the proclamation of the Christian Gospel, had a preparatory character; they prepared the peoples and the nations to receive the new religion, the only true religion. To be sure, this work of Eusebios presents all the merits and defects of all his works. It exhibits his wide erudition, the breadth of his thinking, the wealth of quotations[22] and the comprehensiveness of an excellent historian. One might say that this work is an apology of first quality against the attacks of the learned pagans against Christianity. And one might add that Eusebios surpasses all other apologetic works of antiquity.[23] Of course here too are the defects of his method. The division of his work is not always clear and distinct; sometimes he overlaps his thought with his material and he fails at times to control the balance between the rich material he uses and his own contribution. But all these defects are overwhelmed by the fact that this book is almost as important to us in the study of ancient philosophy exactly as the *Chronikon* and his *Ecclesiastical History* are important for the study of history.

Let us proceed now to a closer examination of Eusebios's thought in reference to his theology of history. If we wanted to summarize in one sentence the basic notion which underlies the present work of Eusebios, this sentence would be "God in History." From the very beginning, Eusebios asks his reader, "Is not he both the dispenser and provider to all men of life and light and truth and all things good? Does he not contain in himself the cause of the being and the life of all things?. . . Or who can be superior to him who claims in the place of a father and a guardian the great President (προστάτην) and absolute Monarch of the universe?[24] It is obvious therefore from the very beginning that for him God is the creator and the cause, and the provider of all things and of all human beings. There is no doubt in Eusebios' mind. Because, "the Word of God sent down from above, like a ray of infinite light, from the God of all goodness proclaims as good tidings to all men; and urges them to come not from this or that place but from every part out of all nations to the God of the universe, and to hasten and accept the gift with all eagerness of soul, Greeks and barbarians together, men and women, and children, both rich and poor, wise and simple, not deeming even slaves unworthy of his call."[25] Apparently, Eusebios appears here as having assimilated completely in his heart and in his mind the Christian conception of equality in every respect. In front of the redemptive task of the Lord all are equal. This is the greatest revolutionary contribution in the historical development of civilization. Further, Eusebios appears quite universal in his conception of history. He writes, "For indeed their Father, having constituted them all of one essence and nature, rightly admitted them all to share in His one equal bounty. . ."[26] But in order to support this thesis, one must be absolutely sure that he stands on solid ground. That is to say, one must be sure that his religion, his theology is sound, true, divine. And beyond any doubt, Eusebios is absolutely sure and positive of that. For he states flatly: "All the circumstances then confirm the story of the facts of our religion, and show that it was not contrived from any human impulse, but divinely foreknown, and divinely announced beforehand by the written oracles (ἐγγράφων χρησμῶν) and yet far more divinely preferred to all men by our Savior."[27] Establishing thus the historical fact of the Christian religion, Eusebios proceeds to prove that great conception which is found in all his works. Simply that the struggle in history is the struggle between the demons and God. The cause of all evils in humanity should be found where else than in the demons? Any specific proof? The wars. Who causes the wars? Eusebios answers: "Surely there is good cause, when one considers it, to wonder why of old, when the demons tyrannized over all the nations, and men paid them much worship, they were goaded by the gods themselves into the furious wars against each other—so that now Greeks were at wars with Greeks, and now Egyptians with Egyptians, and Syrians with Syrians, and Romans with Romans, and made slaves of each other and wore each other out with sieges, as in the fact the histories of the ancients on these matters show."[28] Nevertheless, the demons were defeated ". . .with our Savior's most religious (and peaceful) teaching the destruction of polytheistic error began to be accomplished, and the dissensions of the nations at once to find the rest from the former troubles. This especially I consider to be a very great proof of the divine and irresistable power of our Savior."[29]

Commenting on the religious and spiritual decline and decay of the pagans, Eusebios accepts that the Hebrews worshipped the true God, while the pagans fell to polytheistic idolatry. He says, ". . . few men mentioned among the Hebrews, who with clearest mental eyes looked beyond all the visible world, and worshipped the Maker and Creator of the universe, marvelling much at the greatness of his wisdom and power, which they represented to themselves from his works; and being persuaded that he alone was God, they naturally spoke only of him as God, son from father successively receiving and guiding this as the true, the first, and the only religion."[30] On the contrary, "the rest of mankind, however, fallen away from the only true religion, and gazing in awe upon the luminaries of heaven with eyes of flesh, as mere children in mind, proclaimed them gods, and honoured them with sacrifices and acts of worship. . ."[31] "And accordingly so great a mental paralysis possessed them, that they took no account of the inquities of those whom they regarded as gods, nor blushed at the shameful tales reported of them, but in all these things admired the men because of the benefits provided by them, or because of the governments and tyrannies which were then first established."[32] No doubt, Eusebios grasped the drama of paganism in all its tragic form. But to grasp the drama and the inward meaning of a failure is quite easier than to have to give an answer in order to heal this failure. Eusebios is sure that in this case too, he knows the answer. "Must not then the gospel of Jesus our Savior, the Christ of God, be great and admirable, as teaching all mankind to worship with befitting thoughts the God and Lord of the sun and moon, and Maker of the whole cosmos, who himself high above and beyond the universe, and to celebrate in hymns not the elements of bodies, but him who is the sustainer of life itself, and dispenser of all good things."[33]

Eusebios also touches courageously on the problem of fatalism. He finds that the idea of fatalism comes straight from the demons. He writes:

"So when the demon had by his oracular answers made everything de-
pend on fate, and had taken away the freedom arising from self-
dependence on fate, and had taken away the freedom arising from self-
determined action, and subjugated this also to necessity, see into what
a deadly pit of evil doctrine he had plunged those who believe him."[34]
Eusebios skillfully and wisely overthrows the arguments of the pagans
who supported the blind fatalism in the world and human affairs. Fatalism
is against reason, against the experience of people and against history.
"For if we must refer not only external events, but also the desires founded upon reason, to the stars and fate, and if human judgments are exhorted by some inexorable necessity, there will be an end of your
philosophy, an end also of religion: nor is there, as we thought any praise
of virtue for the good, nor any friendship with God, nor any worthy fruit
of self-denying toils, if universal causation has been usurped by necessity and fate."[35] It becomes obvious that Eusebios is a supporter of the
free-will theory. Proceeding through a series of logical arguments, he
concludes, that, "So evident therefore is the argument for the free will
that, in the same way as the feeling of pain and pleasure, and seeing
and hearing this or that, is perceived not by reasoning but by actual sen-
sation, so we consciously feel ourselves, moving of ourselves and of our
purpose, and choosing some things and rejecting others; thus the freedom
and independence of the rational an intelligent nature in us in any case
justly to be acknowledged."[36] Thus Eusebios expresses his respect for
the human personality and to its divine gift of having the power for move
freelly as a truly rational entity, determining its own life. Of course, this
free-will theory does not come in contrast with the divine providence.
Not at all. "For the soul having obtained this excellent gift from God
is free and master of itself, having assumend the determination of its
own motion: but divine law united with it by nature, like a beacon and
star, call to it with a voice from within and says, "Thou shalt walk in
the king's highway, thou shalt not turn aside to the right hand nor to
the left" teaching us that "the king's highway" is the path in accordance with right reason."[37]

So much from the "Preparation for the Gospel," which, as we have
said, is an apology of the Christian religion against the pagans. But what
about the Hebrews? Eusebios answers them in this book which is called
the "Proof for the Gospel."[38] As a matter of fact, this book is the second part of one book which he called the "Demostration of the
Gospel."[39] But Eusebios answers not only the Hebrews but he also
speaks to the Christians, trying to prove that all the events which accompanied and followed the establishment of the Church are nothing more

than the realization of all the past hopes, the past prophecies, the past expectations. And Eusebios' main point here is that Christianity is the legitimate successor and the natural and physical continuity of the Jewish religion. Besides, Moses and the prophets of the Jewish nation foretold the coming of our Savior and all the events which are connected with his works and the spread of his Gospel. Moreover, all the events which we are now witnessing were foretold by these men, and their prophecies were fulfiled completely. "They are fulfiled in countless and all kinds of ways, and amid all circumstances, both generally and in minute detail, in the lives of individual men, and in their corporate life, now nationally in the course of Hebrew history, and now in foreign nations."[40] Here Eusebios took again the universalistic attitude and interpretation of the events. The prophecies embrace both the Hebrews and the pagans. But he proceeds more specifically and assures his readers that the prophets "said that Christ (whom they named) the Word of God, and himself both God and Lord, and Angel of Great Counsel, would one day dwell among men, and would become for all the nations of he world, both Greek and barbarian, a teacher of true knowledge of God, and of such duty to God Maker of the Universe, as the preaching of the Gospel includes. They said that he would become a little child, and would be called the Son of Man, as born in the race of mankind . . . "[41] " . . . As if they stole a march on history, these same writers proclaimed the very time of his appearance, the precise period of his sojourn on earth."[42] There is no doubt and it is beyond any question that the coming of Christ on the earth was a historical fact. But the majestic things, the astonishing thing, was the historical fact that it was not something new in the strict sense of the word; not at all. The roots of Christianity are planted in the past but "is neither a form of Hellenism, nor of Judaism, but that it is a religion with its own characteristic stamp, and that this is not anything novel or original, but something of the greatest antiquity, something natural and familiar to the godly men before the times of Moses who are remembered for their holiness and justice."[43] Thus, Eusebios clears up misunderstandings which probably would appear and interpret Christianity as a sect of Hellenistic or Jewish descent. The balance between the past and the present, between the new and the old, always preoccupies Eusebios. He then writes, "Christianity would therefore be not a form of Hellenism or of Judaism, but something between the two, the most ancient organization for holiness, and the most venerable philosophy, only lately codified as the law for all mankind in the whole world."[46] However, on what basis could Eusebios argue and support the uniqueness of Christianity. But the question could take another form. Who founded

Christianity? And the answer comes naturally: "It is quite certain that the name "Christian" derived from the name of the Christ of God."[47] Christ then is the founder of Christianity. And Christ, is "our Lord and Savior Jesus Christ. For his kingdom and its throne will stand as long as the sun. And he alone of men, as the Word of God, existed before the moon and the creation of the world, and he alone came down like dew from heaven of all the earth . . . He had risen on all men and that his justice would remain even until the consummation of life, which is called the removal of the moon."[48] It is clear from this passage that Eusebios held the preexistence of Christ before the creation. "The scope of the theology we are considering," Eusebios writes, "far transcends all illustrations, and is not connected with anything physical, but imagines with the acutest thought a Son begotten, not at one time non-existent, and existent at another afterwards, but existent before eternal time, and pre-existent, and ever with the Father as his son, and yet not unbegotten, but begotten from the Father unbegotten, being the only begotten, the Word, and God of God, who teaches that he was not forth from the being of the Father by separation or scission, or division, but unspeakably and unthinkably to us brought into being from all time, nay rather before all times, by the Father's transcendent and inconceivable will and power."[49] Obviously enough, Eusebios accepts this pre-existence of Christ in terms of the created time. Christ of course is before, and above and over our time. He is above history. To be sure, Eusebios realizes the difficulty which arises concerning time in relation with the eternal existence of Christ. But though eternity and time would be defined as two different dimensions, however, in God's plan they are not in contrast and opposition to each other. "For if there is life in things that exist, that life what was begotten in him, for from him and through him is the life-power and the soul-power of all things."[50] Moreover, the Lord in order to care for the sick human souls and provide for their salvation, "He did not even refuse the way of incarnation . . . And he led the life which we lead, in no way foresaking the being that He had before, and ever in the manhood retaining the divinity."[51] There is no doubt therefore that Eusebios tries hard to reconcile time and eternity. Because, in Eusebios' mind, as we have already said, it was clear that historical time is not as such in contrast with the eternal plans of God. On the contrary, with the incarnation of Christ, time was subjected thoroughly to the will of the pre-existent Christ.[52]

The *Ecclessiastical History*[53] is in effect the culmination and climax of the productive mind and pen of Eusebios. It is this work which has given him fame and prestige and the name of the Father of the Ecclesiastical History. A. C. McGiffert has already observed that "Had he written nothing else, Eusebios' *Church History* would have made him immortal; for if immortality be a fitting reward for large and lasting services, few possess a clearer style of Eusebios is here again not under his control, though he writes in an irregular and anomalous fashion and his expressions are not always clear and his ideas and his descriptions are many times repetitions nevertheless, he writes with scientific accuracy, objective criticism and with a vast and admirable knowledge of sources and documents. Most information which we have concerning the early Church is owed to Eusebios. Documents and details which would be lost totally are preserved by him. Of course, the purpose of his Ecclessiastical History is apologetic. He wanted to present to his contemporaries as well as to all generations which would follow, the miracle, that is the astonishing and joyful victory of the Christian Church, after the persecutions and the fears and the contempt of four centuries. One may say without hesitation that he succeeded absolutely in his purpose. He wrote as an historian, taking up himself the full responsibility of a scholar and his most delicate mission. His research is thorough and many modern historians have only admiration for the old man of Caesarea who undertook such a task without the comforts and the facilities which our modern civilization offers. Of course if we judge him by our modern standards of research and of critical analysis, we may find him somewhat behind our way of judging and evaluating historical facts and documents. However, we must keep in mind always the circumstances under which he wrote and we may say that one of his great achievements is that he could, most of the time, distinguish between reliable and unreliable sources and documents. And who can really deny the honesty, and the sincerity of Eusebios? As a master of fact the *Ecclesiastical History* of Eusebios shows the honest motives which inspired him as an historian and a scholar. Because, he undertook a task which really demanded exhaustive research, a truly sharp mind and the critical ability to build up the scheme of the history of the Church, whose history never had been written before. In every way the *Ecclesiastical History* of Eusebios is a precious source for our own research. His theology concerning history is more clear-cut here. His thought expressed in the ten books of his church history are the resume of a tremendous experience, an experience which he lived in the stormy period of the fourth century. The first book especially will be the center of our research.

What is the starting point of Eusebios' *Ecclesiastical History*? He gives the answer himself. "My starting point is no other than the first dispensation of God touching our Savior and Lord, Jesus Christ."[53] It is obvious, therefore that Eusebios, following the straightforward or the "linear" method of writing history, puts down the premise on which he will build his scheme of history. Nevertheless, Eusebios realizes that to begin with Christ is not an easy task. For he has to deal with his "ascription of divinity."[54] Therefore "No treatise, indeed, could be sufficient for a statement of the origin and dignity, the very being and nature of the Christ.[55] Then he proceeds to describe the relation of Christ with his Father and the relation of Christ with the world. "And who, except the Father, would ever clearly conceive the antemundane light, and that wisdom which was intellectual and real before the ages, the living Logos who was, in the beginning, God by the side of the Father, the first and only offspring of God, before all creation and fabrication, both visible and unvisible, the captain of the spiritual and immortal host of heaven, the angel of great counsel, the minister of the ineffable plan of the Father, the fabricator of all things along with the Father,[56] the true and only begotten child of God, the Lord and God and king of all begotten, who has received lordship and might, together with deity itself, and power and honor from the Father, according to the mysterious ascription of divinity to him in the Scriptures."[57] No doubt, Eusebios uses here strong expressions in describing the qualities of the Son. Nevertheless, we can detect again under some words, as for example "minister" (ὑπουργὸν) or "he received lordship and deity" as some hints of the "subordinate" theory of Origen which so much has influenced Eusebios. He accepts the existence of a plan of the creation, as a matter of fact, a dynamic plan which is ministered by Christ and which is a proof of the pre-existence of the second Person of the Trinity as well as of his deity since he is Co-Creator and God by the side of the Father. Just a few lines below, Eusebios adds that "the creator and the fabricator of all things gave up to the Christ himself, and to no other than his divine and first-born Logos, the making of subordinate things and communed with him concerning the creation of man."[58] Plainly therefore, Eusebios does not accept that Christ is the creator of the world by himself. God the Father gave him the making of all creatures except of man in whose creation the Father and the Son worked together according to the Scriptures, "for God said, let us make man in our image and likeness."[59] God the Father is the "Maker" and "the universal sovereign, commanding by his royal nod."[60] The Divine Logos, i. e. is "secondary to him,

and ministering to his Father's commands."[61] It becomes obvious that
Eusebios tries to find out the balance between his subordinate christology
without damaging the deity of Christ and his role in the creation. Does
he achieve this attempt? Not quite; because diplomacy and compromise
do not always co-exist with the Christian truth. He was faced with one
of the most difficult problems of his time: How could a secondary being
be God? But he failed to provide the proper answer or any answer at
all. Hence, the misunderstandings which he created concerning his personality and his works.

Eusebios soon enters into the drama of human history itself. To be
sure there was at the very beginning the life of the blessedness. But the
first man, "despising the command of God; fell at once to this mortal
and perishable life, and exchanged the former divine delights for this
earth with its curse."[62] The original sin is very clear for Eusebios. Cer-
tainly, he follows the biblical interpretation of history and this must be
known from the very beginning. Eusebios, then, proceeds to describe
the results and the consequences of the original sin. Floods, conflagra-
tions, famines, plagues, wars, thunderbolts prevailed in the world. But
into this tragic situation God selected a certain people, the Hebrews. Their
Law, "became famous and spread among all men like a fragrant
breeze."[63] Indeed the Mosaic Law had a universal influence. Because,
beginning with the Hebrews, "the minds of most of the heathen were
softened by the law-givers and philosophers who arose every where."[64]
So, after a period of preparation the "divine and heavenly Logos of God
. . . appeared at the beginning of the Roman Empire through man."[65]
To sum up Eusebios' conception of history: creation, fall, punishment,
preparation, Christ. It is obvious again that Eusebios follows the straight
line of interpretation of history. But if the beginning of his history is
Christ himself, we must keep in mind that his incarnation, his whole
redemptive task is the center of the world history. Because, there is history
before Christ which leads us straight down to the creation of the world.
There is history after the Incarnation, because, here is the Church of
Christ which has a universal character and purpose. Eusebios deals in
reality with the second part of history, the history of the Church which
begins with the coming of Christ on the earth. He is anxious to prove
the historicity of the Incarnation. He refers to prophecies as well as to
persons and events which have direct and immediate historical ralation
with the Incarnation. And then he concludes: "The points suffice as
preliminary observations necessary to establish the truth of the date."[66]
And history proceeds. "Thus by the power and assistance of Heaven the
saving word began to flood the whole world with light like the ray of

the sun . . . In every city and village arose churches crowded with
thousands of men, like a teeming threshing."[67] Thus for Eusebios the
Church becomes afterwards the natural continuation of history. Through
the Church, history will proceed according to the plans of God. "And
now henceforth a day bright and radiant with rays of heavenly light, over-
shadowed by never a cloud, shone down upon the churches of Christ
throughout the whole world."[68] This is really a paean of victory. And
Eusebios understood the victory of the Church, as the most promising
song for the history to come. The great historian of the Church thus
foretold the great impact which the Church will have in the formation
of history. Or we may say that for Eusebios, the church and history are
identified as one stream which runs under the eye of God towards its
great destination.[69]

Before we finish the present work we should cast a glance at a controversial work of Eusebios, i.e. the *Life of Constantine*.[70] Schaff
observed that in this work Eusebios "has almost entirely forgotten the
dignity of the historian in the zeal of the panegyrist."[71] The criticism
is not new at all. Socrates already critized Eusebios for his unreasonable
and excessive adulation of the Emperor.[72] Milburn,[73] on the contrary,
tried to understand the spirit of the epoch. There is no doubt, that
Eusebios, as many of his contemporaries, was tremendously captivated
by the figure of Constantine, the noble and great emperor, who after
his astonishing victories against his adversaries, granted Christianity not
only with freedom, but made the new religion his own religion, and
moreover the favorite religion of the state. Besides, most of the modern
scholars agree today that Eusebios contained in the present work genuine documents and he worked from genuine sourses.[74] But our task
here is to see if the *Life of Constantine* has something to offer to our
scope of research.

We have seen in the previous pages that the fulfilment of history,
according to Eusebios is Christ himself. In him all the prophecies were
fulfilled and through Christ salvation came to the world. But now a new
personality with all the royal majesty comes on the scene. The new personality is Constantine. And there is no doubt that for Eusebios, Constantine the Great is also elected and anointed by God in order to fulfil
His eternal plan, which includes, of course, the victory and dissemina-
tion of the glorious establishment of the Christian Church. Having that
in mind, we could understand the extremely exuberant language which
Eusebios uses. Indeed, for Eusebios, "God himself, . . . has distinguished
him (Constantine) alone of all the sovereigns of whom we have ever heard
as at once a mighty luminary and most clear-voiced herald of genuine

piety.''[75] Moreover God, ''pleased to make him a representative of his own sovereign power, he displayed him as the conqueror of the whole race of tyrants . . .''[76] He compares him with Cyrus, the king of Persians, Alexander the Great, Moses, God! ''The Supreme Governor of the whole universe, by his own will appointed Constantine, the descendant of so renowned a parent, to be prince and sovereign: so that, while others have been raised to this distinction by the election of their fellowmen, he is the only one to whose elevation no mortal may boast of having contributed.''[77] It is obvious, therefore, that for Eusebios, Constantine played a great role in the course of the history of the Church. Besides, Eusebios inclines to connect and identify here, the Church and State under the supreme direction of the emperor. Especially in the tenth chapter of his ''Oration'' in praise of the emperor, Eusebios seems to confuse the relations and the limits in which Church and State could move and live. He speaks of the emperor as the ''interpreter of the Almighty Sovereign's will,''[78] who invites his subjects in every country to the knowledge of the true God. Under Constantine's reign, all the nations of the East and the West are united in praising the one God, the Supreme God. Moreover, Eusebios does not hesitate to call a supper at the Imperial Palace, in which clergymen participated, as ''a picture of Christ's kingdom,''[79] while Constantine himself, entering the assembly of the First Ecumenical Council, appeared ''like some heavenly messenger of God.''[80] Professor Williams of Harvard, in an excellent article published not long ago, tried to prove that there is a connection between the semi-Arian convictions of Eusebios and the exaltations of the Emperor's role, as well as the role of the Empire as such in the scheme of the new Christian era. Indeed, Eusebios holds a low conception concerning the Church as such, and his weak christology as well may have led to an overestimation of the role which the Empire and the emperor could possibly play in the formation of the new era. Truly, this is one of the defects which Eusebios presents in the ''Life of Constantine'' and the ''Oration.'' However we must keep in mind that the ecclesio-political conditions of the fourth century were indeed under the impact of a revolutionary change. The State itself, yesterday's irreconcilable and relentless enemy and persecutor of Christianity, was becoming its chief supporter. This fact was astonishing in every respect. And probably, Eusebios, still under the magnetic and glorious royal mantle, saw the hand of God, Who through Constantine was opening a new road for the Church. Besides, the Roman tradition of the close relations of religion and state very much influenced Eusebios and many of his contemporaries, who saw in Constantine, peace, freedom and wholehearted support.

We have examined in this work, as briefly as possible, the conceptions of Eusebios on the theology of history as they appear in his most important works. Indeed, Eusebios' works hide a great number of merits as well as a considerable number of defects. Nonetheless, however, the student of Eusebios will find in his writings the charm and the attraction which the remote past can always offer. Especially, in Eusebios, the past is present with a pure scientific method, with critical analysis and sufficient judgment. But Eusebios' theology of history is also very important because in many respects he expresses the spirit of his time, and since he was inclining towards semi-Arianism, at least he expresses the spirit of many of his contemporaries. To be sure, his semi-Arian tendencies, his weak christology and ecclesiology influenced the whole construction of his thought. His "subordinatio" theory is obvious everywhere, and bears witness to the influence of Origen upon him. Besides, his eschatology is very dim, or does not exist at all. His ecclesio-political notions bear the impact of the astonishment which overcame him when he saw and witnessed the royal crown come in close relations with the thorny crown of Christ.

Does not all this mean that Eusebios could not construct and form his theology of history? Not at all. He conceived completely the inward meaning of history and with the intuition of an extremely learned and pious historian succeeded in penetrating the very substance of historical procedure. To be sure, he follows the biblical interpretation of history. That is to say, he proceeds on a straight line development of the historical events, which have a special place and goal in the purposeful plan of the divine providence. Eusebios is positive of the pre-existence of Christ before the creation, through whom God the Father created the world, without this "through" to denote a passive attitude. Eternity and history are not in conflict for Eusebios, since both are under the same powerful hand of God. Besides, history is not something abstract in Eusebios' mind. On the contrary, history for him is a concrete entity, has God as its source, and its cause and in reality is universal. The center of history is the "economy" of God, that is to say, the sending of his beloved Son on the earth for the salvation of mankind. Past and future are moving around this center. The Mosaic Law had a preparatory character and it is now out of date. All the prophecies were fulfilled in the person of Christ. His Church continues the unbroken process of history through eternity (since eternity includes history). Thus, the unfolding of all the events must be interpreted under the scope of undeviating development, which takes place under the eye of God.

Eusebios' approach to history is generally sound. It is realistic, well linked, and well developed. Though one may have many points on which to disagree, one can hardly disagree that Eusebios' approach and interpretation of history comes out and flows from the heart and the mind of a man who dedicated himself, with love and passion, to the study and the research of history.

NOTES

[1]Georges Florovsky, "The Predicament of the Christian Historian," in *Religion and Culture: Essays in honor of Paul Tillich*, Walter Leibrecht (New York, 1959), pp. 155 and 161. See also my work: "The Task and the Mission of the Christian Historian according to Georges Florovsky" (in Greek), Θεολογία 32 (1961), 140 ff.

[2]G. La Piana, "Theology of History," *The Interpretation of History* (Princeton, 1943), p. 152.

[3]*Dictionary of Christian Biography*, 2, p. 345.

[4]It has been the custom to identify and compare Eusebios with Herodotos, the father of history. R. L. P. Milburn, in his book: *Early Christian Interpretations of History* (London, 1954), p. 62, prefers to compare Eusebios with the Jewish historian Josephus (A.D. 37-100). Among other reasons, Milburn argues that both write with an apologetic motive, both make careful use of documents.

[5]For the life of Eusebios see Hieronymus, *De viris illustribus*, c. 81. Valesius, *De vita scriptisque Eusebii Caesar*. F. C. Baur, *Comparatur Eusebios his. eccl. parents cum parente hist. Herodoto* (Tübingen, 1834). Lyman Coleman, *Eusebios as an Historian*, in the *Bibliotheca Sacra* (Andover, 1858), pp. 78-96. J. B. Lightfoot, in the *Dictionary of Cristian Biography* 2, pp. 308-48 . F. J. Stein, *Eusebios, Bischof von Caesarea* (Würzburg, 1859). J. Stevenson, *Studies in Eusevios* (Cambridge, 1929). F. J. Foakes-Jackson, *Eusebios Pamheli* (Cambridge, 1933). D. S. Balanos, *Patrology* (Athens, 1930). K. Kontogonis, *Philological and Critical History* (Athens, 1906). F. O. Gayre, *Manual of Patrology and History of Theology* (Paris, Tournai, Roma, 1935). Tixeront-Raemers, *Handbook of Patrology* (St. Louis, London, 1951). Ph. Schaff, *History of the Christian Church*, vol. 3, (Grand Rapids, 1953). R. L. P. Milburn, *Early Christian Interpretations of History* (London 1954). For the most recent work and bibliography see Johannes Quasten, *Patrology* (Utrecht/Antwerp, 1960), vol, 3, pp. 309 ff. See also the article on Eusebios in the Θρησκευτικὴ καὶ 'Ηθικὴ 'Εγχυκλοπαιδεία vol. 5, pp. 1078 ff.

[6]The accusation against Eusebios is well known. It was made by Bishop Potamon of Heraclea at the Council of Type (335 or 336) according to whom he had escaped any harm from the imprisonment during the persecution. Most scholars agree today that this is an accusation made in the excitement and bitterness of the controversy. Besides, it remains incomprehensilbe how a "lapsus" could become a bishop of a prominent city.

[7]Ernest Horigmann, *Eusebios Pamphili*; The Removal of his name from the diptychs of the Caesarea in Palestine in 431 A. D. in "Patristic Studies" (Vatican City, 1953), p. 65.

[8]Honigmann concludes that Cyril removed Eusebios' name from the diptychs of the Church of Caesarea on the request of Juvenal, the Bishop of Jerusalem, who wanted to humiliate the Metropolitan under whose jurisdiction he belonged. Thus Cyril secured the help and support of the bishop of Jerusalem in Ephesos. For more details see ibid, pp. 68-70.

[9]Jerome (in his Epistle to Pammachius an Oceanus, Ep. ch and in his Apology against Rufinus, Book 1, chap. 8), Theodoret, (*Eccles. Hist.* 1,5) Epiphanios (*Heresy to the Meletians,* Haer. 68) as well the Acts of the Seventh Ecumenical Council consider Eusebios as an Arian (Mansi, *SS. Conc. Coll,* vol. 13, pp. 316-17). Also Photios (144th Epistle to Constantine and in his *Bibliotheca* chap. 13). Modern scholars as Baronius, Petavius, Clericus, Tillemont, Gieseler, consider him as an Arian. Others, as Mohler (in Athanasius der Grosse, pp. 333ff) consider him as semi-Arian. Also J. Stevenson (*Studies,* p. 136) and G. H. Williams, "Christology and Church State Relation," *Church History,* The Popes Gelasius and Pelagius II and Dr. Sam Lee (in Introduction treatise in his English edition of the *Theophany of Eusebios* (Cambridge, 1843) pp.xxiv-xix, defended the orthodoxy of Eusebios. Many Anglicans do the same. I think the best solution, in this case was given by Prof. D. S. Balanos who refuted the accusations against Eusebios by proving from the study of his anti-Nicene and post Nicene writings that he is not a double-crosser, a double-minded man, or wavering and leaning on both sides. His christological convictions remained the same, which to be true were according to Prof. Balanos akin to the Arian christology. If he defended Arius, in some cases his intentions were inspired from a deep and sincere desire for peace in the Church and the Empire. Cf. Balanos, *The Character of the Ecclesiastical Historian Eusebios* (in Greek) (Athens, 1934). Professor Florovsky, in commenting on Eusebios' letter to Constantia Augusta, the sister of Constantine the Great, a letter with obvious iconoclastic overtones and happily used by the Iconoclasts "post factum," points to the fact that Eusebios was actually an Origenist and we must always bear in mind that Origen's christology was inadequate and ambiguous. See, Georges Florovsky, "Origen, Eusebios, and the Iconoclastic Controversy," *Church History,* 19 (1950) 86 and 87.

[10]See above p. 73, n. 9; cf., G. Florovsky, "Origen."

[11]Eusebios writes himself that, " . . . we shall add to the general history only such things as may be profitable, first to ourselves, and then to those that come after us." (H. E. 7. 2. 3) From this passage Gibbon had drawn conclusion that Eusebios is prejudiced towards Christianity. See, Edward Gibbon, *The Decline and Fall of the Roman Empire* (NY, 1932), 1, p. 501.

Though it is reallly hazardous to claim that a historian could be absolutely objective, nevertheless, Eusebios himself frankly amidst the faults which the Christians had during his time; cf. E.H. 8. 1. 7. ff.

[12]Polybios, 25. 6.

[13]*Eusebios.*

[14]Ibid. p. 62.

[15]*Eusebios, Ecclesiastical History,* (Cambridge), 1, p.xv.

[16]Lightfoot, p. 31.

[17]This work is of course based on the previous effort of Julius Africanus (170-240-250 A. D.), well known as *Chronographia,* The *Chronikon* of Eusebios

was divided into two parts. The first, the *Chronographia*, is an epitome of universal history. It is drawn from various sources and is in tabular form. It is arranged nation by nation and it offers critical discussions of their systems of reckoning dates. Unfortunately ths part is lost except a some unconnected fragments preserved by the Byzantine chronographer Georgios Synkellos. The second part consists of chronological tables with marginal comments and it is in reality a series of parallel columns, one for each great empire. It is called "Chronological Canons." It seems that the *Chronicon* of Eusebios was produced first in 303. But it seems however, that a second edition followed in 325 or a little later. It was translated by Jerome with the addition of more notes and it is a continuation of the chronology down to his own time. The Greek title of the second part is Χρονικῶν κανόνων παντοδαπὴ ἱστορία. The classical work on the *Chronicle* is that of A. Schoene, *Eusebi Chronicorum Libri duo*, vol 1, 1875, vol. II, 1866.

[18]J. Shotwell, *An Introduction to the History of History* (N. Y. 1922), p. 307.

[19]Cf. in Migne PG 19. 103-04.

[20]Migne, PG 19. 355 and 521-23.

[21]The best Greek and English edition of the "Preparation for the Gospel" is that of E. H. Gifford, in four volumes (Oxford, 1903). Cf. also in PG. 21.22 ff. The Greek title is "Εὐσεβίου τοῦ Παμφίλου Εὐαγγ. Προπαρασκευῆς Λόγοι ΙΕ." In reality this work is the first part of one whole work. The second part is "Proof of the Gospel," for which we shall speak later. The work was written probably after 313.

[22]Eusebios in this work included extracts from almost every prominent philosopher many of which would never have survived without Eusebios copying them.

[23]Lightfoot justly states that "There is the same greatness of conception marred by the same inadequacy of execution, the same profusion of learning combined with the same inability to control his materials . . ." McGiffert writes that "the wide acquaintance with classical literature exhibited by Eusebios in the *Preparation* is very remarkable," see *The Church History of Eusebios* in the series of Nicene and post-Nicene Fathers," vol. 1 in the "Prolegomena," p. 34. The quotations are taken from the English translation of F. H. Gifford, *Eusebios Preparation for the Gospel* (Oxford, 1903).

[24]Book 1, chap. 1 p. 2, c and d.

[25]Ibid. p. 3. a.

[26]Ibid. p. 3. b.

[27]Ibid. 4, p. 9. d.

[28]Ibid. p. 10. d.

[29]Ibid. p. 11. a.

[30]Book 1. ch. VI, p. 17, c.

[31]Ibid. chap. 6. p. 17. d.

[32]Book 2, chap. 5, p. 73. c.

[33]Book 3, chap. 6, p. 96. d.

[34]Book 6, chap. 6, p. 242. d.

[35]Book 6, chap. 6, p. 242. d.

[36]Ibid. p. 245. c.

[37]Ibid. p. 250. b.

[38]The Greek title is $Εὐαγγελικὴ$ $Ἀποδείξεως$ $Δέκα$ $Λόγοι$" and the Latin "Demonstratio Evangelica." See the Greek edition in PG 22. 14ff. The best English translation by W J. Ferrar in two volumes ed. (London, NY, 1920). It seems probable that it was written after 303 and before 313, together of course with the *Preparation for the Gospel* Lightfoot characterizes both books as "probably the most important apologetic work of the Early Church" (D. C. B. ii, 329).

[39]*The Preparation for the Gospel*, Book 1 chap. 1, p. 4. a b.

[40]*The Proof for the Gospel*, Book 1, chap. 1, Introduction, 3. The English translation belongs to Ferrar.

[41]Ibid. chap. 1.4.

[42]Ibid.

[43]Ibid. chap. 2.12.

[44]Ibid. chap.2.14.

[45]6. chap. 18.294C.

[46]7. chap. 3.354.d,355a.

[47]4. chap. 3.149.a.

[48]Ibid. chap. 5.150.C.

[49]Ibid. Chap. 10.165. B and C.

[50]We have already mentioned the problem concerning the relation of God the Father with the Son. Here, it seems that Eusebios follows the theory of subordination, according to which the second Person of the Trinity, Christ, is "a secondary being" (Book 1, chap. 5.11.b), "Lord in the second degree," (Book 4, chap. 7, 156, c.) and "co-operating in his Father's commands . . . and stands midway the unbegotten God and the things after him begotten. . ." (Book 4, 10, 164, c.d.). Here of course the influence of Origen is obvious. It is noteworthy though, that Eusebios' "subordinatio" theory did not affect the firm belief and positive assurance which he had for the redemptive task of Christ and its effects on history. It is unfortunate that from the twenty books of the "Proof of the Gospel" only ten are extant. In the lost ten books we could have the whole development of the apologetic approach of Eusebios concerning the whole scheme of redemptive work of Christ. For a more pertinent discussion of the problem cf. J. Stevenson *Studies in Eusebius*, p. 73ff.

[51]Cf. the Greek text in P.G. 20.45. See also the English translation in the Select Library of Nicene and Post-Nicene Fathers of Ph. Schaff vol. 1, trans. A.C. McGiffert. Also the Greek text of E. Schwartz with the english translation by Prof. K. Lake, in the Loeb Classical Library in two vols. The Greek title $Εὐσεβίου,$ $Ἐκκλησιαστικῆς$ $Ἱστορίας$ $Λόγοι$ $Δέκα.$ The Latin title is *Historia Ecclesiastica*. The earlier printed text of the Ecclesiastical History is that of Stephanos, in Paris, 1544. The later, that of Schwartz, (Leipzig, 1903) reprinted in the Loeb Classical Library in 1926, 1949, 1953. Eusebios wrote this work not at the same time. The first eight books were edited probably after 311; the second edition with the ninth book was probably edited in 315. And the third edition with the tenth book added in 317. See for details and the arguments in the edition of the Loeb Classical Library by Prof. K. Lake.

[52]A.C. McGiffert, *The Church History of Eusebius*, in the Nicene and Post-

Nicene Fathers by Ph. Schaff, vol. 1, p. 46.

[53]H.E. 1.i.2.

[54]Ibid. 1.i.1.

[55]Ibid. 1.ii.2.

[56]Ibid. 1.ii.3. The Greek text adds here: "τὸν δεύτερον μετὰ τὸν Πατέρα τῶν ὅλων αἴτιον." McGiffert translates it more properly. . . "the second cause of the universe after the Father."

[57]H.E. 1.ii.3.

[58]Ibid. 1.ii.4.

[59]From Gen 1.26; H.E. 1,ii,4.

[60]Ibid. 1.ii.5.

[61]Ibid. 1.ii.4. The subordinate tendencies of Eusebios appear also a little below when he writes seeing that it is improper to call him the first cause of the universe. Ibid. 1.ii.8.

[62]Ibid. 1.ii.18.

[63]Ibid. 1.ii.23.

[64]Ibid.

[65]Ibid.

[66]Ibid. 1.vi.ii.

[67]Ibid. 2.ii.1.

[68]Ibid. 10.i.8.

[69]For a more substantial discussion concerning Eusebios' stand on many problems of history see: Jean Sirinelli, *Les Vues Historiques d' Eusèbe de Césarée durant la période Prèniceenne.* Publications de la section de Langues et Litteratures, No. 10 (Dakar, 1961).

[70]The best edition of the "Life" may be considered that of Heinichen, published in 1830 and republished in 1830. We use here the English translation of E.C. Richardson, in the Nicene and Post-Nicene Fathers vol. 1. For the Greek text see PG 909ff.

[71]Ph. Schaff, *History of the Christian Church,* vol. 3, p. 876.

[72]Socrates, H.E.

[73]Milburn, 66ff. For a constructive criticism, see also F.J. Foakes-Jackson, pp. 102ff.

[74]G. Bonis, Eusebios' Pamphili work, *Εἰς τὸν βίον τοῦ Μακαρίου Κωνσταντίνου Βασιλέως,* as a historical document, in Greek (Athens, 1939).

[75]Book 1. Chap. 4.

[76]Ibid. Chap. 5.

[77]Ibid. Chap. 24.

[78]*Oration,* chap. 10.

[79]*The Life,* Book 3, chap. 15.

[80]*The Life,* Book. Ibid. 3, chap. 10.

[81]G.H. Williams, "Christology and Church-State relations in the Fourth

Century." *Church History*. The author in a brilliant way touches a problem which has not been much discussed.

Gregory of Nyssa's *Life of Moses*:
A Philosophical and Theological Analysis

W. Jaejer correctly observed in one of his last works that Gregory of Nyssa in his *Life of Moses* had incorporated his ontology "into the theory of the ascetic life."[1] For Gregory of Nyssa philosophy and ontology had taken a complete new dimension and a profounder meaning. For him the monks are the true philosophers,[2] and the ascetic life is a "whole path of philosophy."[3] Although one might agree with Jaeger that in Gregory the idea of the ascetic life was a parallel and in many ways a direct continuation of the "vita cotemplativa" of the ancient Greek philosophers,[4] one must also accept the fact that in Gregory of Nyssa the ascetic life as a "philosophical life" or as "vita contemplativa" has a different basis and a completely different orientation and purpose. Speaking especially for the *Life of Moses*, one must stress its thorough biblical basis and background, its theological orientation and its soteriological purpose. Here Gregory not only interprets and discusses important passages of the Scriptures. He goes even further by basing his theory on the Christian Scriptures, the Christian ascetic life, on a purely biblical substratum. He presents Moses as the pattern of the continuous spiritual progress, as the prototype of a gradual process of purification of the soul, and as the image of Christ himself. Actually, the whole life of Moses points towards the life of Christ. Moses' extention of arms foreshadowed the mystery of the Cross.[5] The meaning of the spiritual tabernacle shown to Moses (Ex 25-27) is an anticipation of Christ. Taking a small clue from Paul, Saint Gregory writes:

> who has partially revealed the mystery involved here. We shall that by this symbol Moses was instructed in anticipation of the Tabernacle which embraces the universe. And this is Christ, the power and the wisdom of God, who being in his own nature not made by human hands, received a created existence when he was to build his tabernacle among us. Thus the same tabernacle is in a certain sense, both created and uncreated: uncreated in his pre-existence, he recieved a created subsistence precisely in this material tabernacle.[6]

Moreover, the rock that God spoke to Moses about " . . . is Christ, who is all perfection. . ."[7]

Then the theological orientation of the *Life of Moses* is more than obvious. Saint Gregory is interested here in proving how important it " . . . is to learn how to follow the Lord,"[8] or in seeing God which means "following him wherever he might lead,"[9] even in entering "into the darkness and of the vision of God."[10]

This purely theological orientation does not fully exclude Gregory's interest in human knowledge and in human categories even in Greek philosophy and speculation. He uses sometime without caution the traditional relation of theology and human speculation. There is no doubt that the problem of the relation between philosophy and theology is an acute one in most of the works of Gregory of Nyssa. Here H. Cherniss's monograph on *The Platonism of Gregory of Nyssa*[11] still remains original and valuable. Cherniss maintains that "the strongest link between Plato and Gregory and the most important characteristic of the system of the latter for the history of philosophy is the acceptance by him of the fundamental metaphysical ideas of Plato and his constant adherence thereto."[12] He also thinks that Gregory not only failed to improve Platonism by applying and adjusting its ideas and intentions into the framework of Christian problematics, but that he also was full of contradictions; that he would be orthodox at any cost of intellectual integrity; that he was a man of double nature so penetrating in thought and so perverse in drawing his conclusions, that he was even ready to show "the scourging tongue of the righteous servant of the Church, pointing with one hand of scorn at Eunomios for using the arguments of Aristotle and Plato while with the other he filched the same source."[18]

Cherniss's harsh criticism is unjust. That Gregory was a man of erudition, that his true intellectual interests had been with Greek philosophy and poetry, that he uses Platonic terminology in expounding his theological thought — all these are facts which no serious student of Gregory can dispute with. Even in his *Life of Moses,* the descriptions he gives of God indicate the knowldge of the Platonic theology.[14] That at times he might have experienced "an acute civil war within himself," as Cherniss maintains, this also might be true. Indeed, one might legitimately detect in his writings a stern tension between the man of letters and the man of religion, between the man of speculation and the man of faith. But it is not a matter of conjecture to ascertain that in most of his works and specifically in his *Life of Moses*, he manages finally to overcome this inner tension in order to prove himself a true and faithful Christian thinker. Thus he is more than eager to point out the true value of the pagan and secular knowledge and its proper setting in the divine scheme of Christian salvation. To be sure, pagan and secular knowledge is "a spouse of foreign stock,"[15] and moreover, pagan philosophy is "childless . . . always in pains of childbirth it never engenders living offspring. What fruit has philosophy brought forth worthy of such labor? Are not all [its] fruits inane and undeveloped and miscarried before they enter the light of the knowledge of God?"[16] Gregory's main contention, therefore, is that Greek philosophy or secular knowledge is sterile in itself.[17] Thus he defends himself against those who fervently criticized him for his personal and quite emotional attachment to the Greek culture. In fact, the life of Moses offers him a fine biblical allegory for the place of Greek philosophy in the scheme of the biblical theology of history. The wooden box in which the infant Moses drifted on the waters of the Nile means for him the "composite system of secular learning"[18] and the sterility of pagan philosophy in general is embodied in the figure of Pharaoh's daughter, who, since she cannot give life to a child of her own, eagerly adopts the Jewish infant she finds exposed in the wooden box on the waters of the Nile.[19] But beyond this critical evaluation of pagan learning, Gregory attempts to bridge the existing gap which separates Greek philosophy and Christian faith. He not only subordinates the first to the latter, he not only examines the pagan learning, through the authority of the Scriptures, but at the same time he is consistent in his effort to bring about "the catharsis of Greek philosophy" as Professor Jaeger has already noted;[20] further, he is ready to recognize its real value and actually to employ it in the service of Christian life. He writes: "For there is, indeed, something in pagan learning which is worthy of being united to us for the purpose of engendering virtue. It must not be rejected. For the philosophy of both ethics and nature may well become consort, friend and life-companion of the higher life, if only which is born of her bring with itself nothing of the foreign stain."[21]

This attitude of Gregory of Nyssa on Greek philosophy and the pagan learning in general is most significant because it is expressed in his *Life of Moses*, a work which he completed near the end of his life. He speaks about his white hair[22] and he leaves the impression that he writes as a man of experience and senile prudence. One might say that *Life of Moses* is the recapitulation of Gregory's religious experience, the crystallization of his theological insights, and the confirmation of his standing as far as the relation of philosophy and theology is concerned,[23] So here we find not only "a satisfactory formulation of the relationship of Christian theology to Greek philosophy,"[24] but also we face a man of

profound ascetical ideals and convictions who was able to reach an
equilibrium between human categories and divine Revelation and who,
with absolute personal integrity, could claim simultaneously that although
pagan learning is σαρκώδης τε καὶ ἀλλόφυλος, its acquisition is a divine
commandment.[26]

Cherniss's case, therefore, against Gregory of Nyssa is not bound
anymore to gain substantial support in view of a careful analysis of *Life
of Moses*. On the contrary, Fr. Danielou's stand on Gregory of Nyssa
has been more serious and more balanced. Fr. Danielou points to the
literary dependence of Gregory on Plato and the adaptation of basic
philosophical concepts to Christian doctrine and in general to biblical
language and terminology.[27] In other words, Danielou's contribution lies
on his assumption that Gregory's motifs were theological and therefore
his "Platonism" is no longer "Platonic" but Christian; and that we can
see here a complete "metamorphosis" of Plato's thought and terminology
into the sphere of Christian theology and ascetic piety.

No serious student of the Fathers of the Church in general and of
Gregory of Nyssa in particular will disclaim any literary inter-connection
of their thought with classical philosophy. Philosophical conceptions and
philosophical categories have become a common property in the age of
the great Fathers of the Church and were used extensively by Christian
and non-Christian thinkers alike. The most important point, however,
which should be made here is that the use of philosophical language by
Gregory of Nyssa (and the rest of the Fathers) is not a sign of spiritual
indigence and improvisation, but on the contrary, it proves a deep sense
of "historicity," a profound respect for history in which the *magnalis
Dei* (the mighty deeds of God) are intrinsically linked and united in the
great design for the salvation of mankind. The use of Greek philosophy
in the realm of the Christian faith and piety should be interpreted in
the light of the historical continuity of Christianity and as an imperative
testimony of Christianity's dimension towards the past. This is why
Gregory of Nyssa speaks of the secular learning as πλοῦτος (wealth and
treasure) which in due time was offered as gift and as ornament to the
Church of God. Ethics, physics, geometry, astronomy, logic — all should
beautify the "divine temple of the mystery" and the monks who live
now the "life of freedom" should prepare "themselves in their spiritual
life with the "ἔξωθεν παίδευσιν."[28]

Church and paideia, ascetic life and mental discipline, faith and
speculation do not exclude each other but should be interpreted as meaningful signs of the existing unity of history. Gregory is well aware of the

value of history in the perspective of his biblical theology and hermeneutics. In his *Life of Moses* he repeatedly speaks about the life of Moses as an ἱστορία[29] absolutely reliable and trustworthy; and although one might see in the ἱστορία the works of evil,[30] he is also reminded that through the events of this ἱστορία we are constantly educated and edified in our spiritual endeavors.[31] One might object at this point that the term ἱστορία should be construed as simply a "story"; but precisely in the unfolding events of this "story," Gregory of Nyssa can see all the development of a continuous fight between God and Satan, between good and evil.[32] Thus a history-minded man like Gregory of Nyssa could not but look at "Greek paideia" as an unavoidable phenomenon in the concrete and universal progress of time, as an organic part in the Christian vision of history.

Dr. Daniélou has rightly singled out the profound spirituality of Gregory's works, the inner mystical meaning of his ascetic theology, and the vigilant "apatheia" in the contemplation of the Divine.[33] All these elements also abound in *The Life of Moses* and we shall speak about them a little later.

One must also not lose sight of two other important aspects of Gregory's work and especially of his *De Vita Moysis;* these are the christological and soteriological basis and orientation. Only through the christological and soteriological perspective could the ascetical theology of Gregory of Nyssa be understood and evaluated.

Thus Christ and salvation through Christ are central and most important concerns of Gregory in his *De Vita Moysis*. Moses himself is the image or the prototype, the τύπος of Jesus Christ.[34] The two stone "tablets of testimony" which Moses brought down from Mount Sinai and broke into pieces are symbols of our flesh and the flesh the Lord took when he became man.[35] The finger of God which wrote the commandments upon the two stone tablets is a symbol of the Holy Spirit which came upon the Virgin Mary,[36] the burning bush is again the Virgin Mary, who although she gave birth to Jesus Christ, remained incorruptible;[37] the light in the bush is Christ himself;[38] the manna rained down from heaven is a miracle which "serves to instruct us by foreshadowing the mystery of the Virgin; for this bread that does not come from earth is the Word, who with varying degrees of perfection adapts his effects to the dispositions of those who receive him.[39] The rock in Choreb (Ex 17.6) is a symbol of Christ himself.[40] The lifting up of the serpent in the wilderness (Num 21.9) as well as the raised hands of Moses

represent the Cross;[41] the passing through the Red Sea (Ex 14.27-30) is
an image of the Christian baptism; it is the "mystic washing," the "life-
giving for those who take refuge in it . . .",[42] and as the Israelites crossed the Red Sea with the guidance of the cloud, the same way we shall
cross the water of baptism, with the Holy Spirit as guide securing
"redemption, burying in the sea the one who pursues to enslave us."[43]
"So, too, in this episode," Saint Gregory concludes, "we ordered to drown
every Egyptian, that is, every form of sin, in the saving waters of baptism as in the depths of the sea, and then emerge from the waters alone
without allowing anything foreign to trail us into our life."[44] The bough
and the cluster of grape which the messengers brought back to Moses
from the land of Canaan (Num 13.23), as well as the "wine, the blood
of the grape," which Israel drank in the wilderness (Deut. 32.14) symbolize the σωτήριον πάθος of Christ and the σωτήριον ποτόν, that is, the
holy eucharist.[45] Also the twelve springs the Israelites found in Elim,
together with the seventy stems of palm trees (Ex 15.27), have a deeper
meaning. "The springs are the twelve Apostles whom our Lord chose
for this purpose, making his word rise up through them as from a spring
. . . And the seventy palm trees would, of course, be those Apostles who
were chosen over and above the Twelve and sent out into the whole world;
for these were of the same number as the palm trees in the text" (Lk
10.1).[46]

   To a man not familiar with the patristic tradition, all these might
seem as sheer imaginary or rigid and aimless symbolism. However, Saint
Gregory is not a captive of his symbolism. He is a pragmatist, a historian,
who behind the events of history can read the present and the future.
He knows how to read "documents of life," "intelligible documents,"[47]
that is, historical sources to which he knows how to respond and establish
inner relationship and affinity. Actually, in his *Life of Moses*, Saint
Gregory managed to grasp the inherent meaning of the biblical history,
to put the story of Moses in the proper perspective of salvation and to
interpret it in the context of the New Testament experience. We might
say then, that this experience is not simply "existential" but rather a
soteriological experience, an new dimension of ultimate character which
is manifested in the person of Jesus Christ. In other words, Saint
Gregory's main interest is the salvation of mankind through Jesus Christ
our Lord.

   Thus he always is ready to point out that ". . . it was for our sake
that he accepted to be born among us, who had lost existence by the
abuse of freedom, that he might restore to existence all that had gone
astray from it . . ."[48] Only in Christ we shall find the true resting place

for " . . . indeed, the Only-begotten, by whom all things were made, is himself the place for those who run; he is, according to his own words, the very way of the course, as well as the rock for those who are well grounded, and the mansion for those who take their rest . . ."[49] This is why Gregory never fails to look at Christ as "the Author of our salvation"[50] and his blood as "draught of salvation to those that drink it."[51]

Yet the doctrine of salvation is not fully understood unless it can be seen through the perspective of human freedom. Freedom, ἐλευθερία, is for Gregory of Nyssa the indispensable condition upon which the ascetic life — all Christian life — can be sustained and lived. Again and again he points to the fact that the mystery of Incarnation, which is depicted through the burning bush, aimed at the abolishment of the tyrant (that is, Satan) and the liberation of all those who were captive under his tyrannical and oppressive dominion.[52] Speaking about the deadly serpents which bit the people of Israel in the wilderness (Num 21.6-7), he reminds us that they depict our sins from which Christ came to liberate us.[53] Yet this liberation from sins is not easily acquired and kept. It is imperative to struggle unceasingly for it, for even after the sacrament of baptism, we might still be captives of the slavery of sin and still cower before the tyrants of evil.[54] We must drown in the waters of baptism the tyrant of sin; we "must kill in these waters the entire host of sins . . ."[55] Incontinence, impure desires, the spirit of greed and avarice, the feelings of vanity and pride, irascible feelings, anger, wrath, jealously, envy and the like are passions which naturally accompany our human nature, and they are masters and tyrants which we must annihilate in the "mystic water" of baptism not allowing them anymore to trail us into our life.[56] The passions of the human soul are depicted in the story of Moses by the Egyptian army which unsuccessfully tried to stalk the Israelites in the Red Sea; and as the Egyprian army was drowned in the sea and Israel, free from the Egyptian bondage, crossed the sea, so "we ordered to drown every Egyptian, that is every form of sin, in the saving water of baptism as in the depths of the sea . . ." and give up "the Egyptian pleasures" to which we have been enslaved before crossing the water.[57] However, we must always remember that "we cannot be rid of the Egyptian bondage, unless we leave Egypt, that is, this life that lies under water, and pass, not that Red Sea, but this black and gloomy sea of life . . ."[58] In other words, we must cleanse ourselves from the evils of the "Egyptian and foreign life," that is, we must free and disengage ourselves from the fleshly needs and the indulgences of the secular life.[59] Then our lives can be led towards freedom[60] and we might be able to live a "free life," an ἐλεύθερον βίον[61] a life truly sweet and refreshing and pleasant. Saint

Gregory describes this really free life in a most convincing way: "After crossing the sea there followed a three day's march, and during this time they encamped in a place where they found water which they could not at first drink because of its bitter taste (Ex 15.23). But the wood that Moses cast into the water made it a pleasant drink for them in their thirst. The text corresponds with what actually happens: when a man has given up the Egyptian pleasures to which he had been enslaved before crossing the water, his life seems at first bitter and disagreeable now that his pleasures have been taken away. But once the wood is cast into the waters, that is, once he unites to the mystery of the resurrection, which had its beginning in the wood (and by the wood here, you surely understand the Cross), then the life of virtue becomes sweeter and more refreshing than all the sweetness that makes the sense tingle with pleasure, because it has been seasonable by our hope in the things to come."[62]

This life of freedom, of course, is "a life of virtue." It is the life of a continuous ascent, a life of contemplation. Virtue, ascent and contemplation are the trilogy of the ascetic life, the consolidating and sure grounds upon which Gregory bases the mystical life of the Christian, the mystical experience of the incomprehensibility of God. Now, the life of virtue, which is also called "virtue according to piety" or κατ' εὐσέβειαν ἀρετή, has two main charactiristics: first faith in God, or the proper knowledge about God (ἅ χρὴ περὶ τοῦ Θεοῦ γινώσκειν) and, second, the moral achievements, or the purity of life and the good conscience. (Ἡ τοῦ βίου καθαρότης, ἡ κατὰ τὸν βίον τοῦτον ἀγαθὴ συνείδησις.)[63]

This life of virtue is at the same time a life of moderation, the middle way, or the "royal highway" (Num 20.17) from which no deviation is permitted; for any turning away, any aversion towards the sidewalks is indeed dangerous. There are cliffs on both sides of the road of Christian virtue and any mistake can lead to spiritual death. Any definition of the life of virtue should be drawn from the fact that exercise of virtue is a actually a continuous practice of moderation and the avoiding an shunning away deeds of the extremes. Valor as a virtue, for instance, lies between timidity and impudence. Wisdom lies between shrewdness and naivete, temperance between licentiousness and the abhorring of marriage as being an act of adultery. Thus virtue is considered as being in the middle between the extreme evils and by avoiding the extremes, the practice of virtue becomes a mild and sweet habit, a pleasant possession.[64]

And yet to pursue the life of virtue means in reality man's attempt to attain perfection. Virtue and perfection are almost synonyms which describe the mystical participation in God himself; they denote the

mystical experience to know the Highest Good and share in it. But virtue is not having any limit; it is boundless. To stop on the path of virtue
is to begin on the path of evil. What can be contained within the limits
is not virtue, because God is the most perfect and infinite virtue, the
ultimate and sovereign Good without any limit. It becomes obvious,
therefore, that the life of perfection is not having any limit, it is boundless.
Nobody can define perfection, no one can attain perfection.[65] The life
of virtue and the life of perfection are a way of life in the course of which
we must never neglect the divine command, "Be you perfect, as your
heavenly Father is perfect." (Mt 5.48) We must make any effort not to
fall short utterly of the perfection that is possible to us, for indeed human
perfection, the perfection of Christian life consists "in the constant growth
in the good[66]. . . in our never stopping in our growth in good, never cir-
cumscribing our perfection by any limitation."[67]

Here the concept of continuous ascent and constant growth enters
into the framework of Gregory's ascetical theology. The whole ascetic
life is for him toilsome ascent, a ceaseless struggle, a tiresome journey,
which we must carry on in the sweat of our brow. The message we can
draw from Moses's life is precisely this: that the road towards perfection
is a road towards progress, that the ascent towards perfection is a pro-
gressive one and that the perfection of the soul is actually an "incre-
ment" towards moral excellence: "ἀλλ' ἡ πρὸς τὸ κρεῖττον ἀεὶ γινομένη
τοῦ βίου ἐπαύξησις ὁδός ἐστι τῇ ψυχῇ πρὸς τελείωσιν . . ."[68]

Moses' ascent to Mount Sinai and Jacob's ladder provide Saint
Gregory with rich terminology for the description of the spiritual growth
and advancement towards perfection. He calls it ἄπαυστον πρὸς τὰ ἄνω
φοράν or κίνησιν,[69] πρὸς τὰ ἄνω πορείαν,[70] πρόοδον πρὸς τὸ καλὸν[71] and
ἀνωφερῆ καὶ δυσπόρευτον πορείαν ἀρετῆς,[72] or ἄνοδον πρὸς τὸν Θεόν,[73] or
θείαν ἄνοδον[74] and ἄνοδον πρὸς τὸ ὄρος,[75] as well as ἀνάβασιν πρὸς τὰ ὑψη-
λότερα τῆς ἀρετῆς.[76]

Now the question is whether there will be any hindrances in this
spiritual ascent, or whether there will be a final end, a satisfactory limit
to the spiritual road towards perfection. Saint Gregory's answer is une-
quivocally negative. He finds that Moses' ascent to Mount Sinai offers
us a parallel, instructive picture for the constantly required progress in
the ascetic life. "How are we to understand the meaning of this summit
to which the text leads us?" Saint Gregory asks. "For it is this which Moses,
after so many ascents, longed to reach; and He, too, helps us to reach
it by His guidance . . ."[77] Thus it is clear that Moses' ceaseless struggle
and toilsome ascent towards the summit of Mount Sinai has, according
to the words of Saint Gregory, "greater depth and magnificence."[78]

Let us quote here the whole paragraph in which the great Cappadocian Father shows that he knows how to use the allegorical method in interpreting the Bible, a method which transforms the historical essence of the Bible and its pedagogic message into a flowing stream of true spiritual experience, that is, a spiritual reality for those who are eager to live the mystical and ascetic life of the Church. He writes: "I think this idea quite fills all that we have already seen. When God speaks of a place, he does not mean a space that can be quantitatively measured — for we cannot measure anything that does not have quantity — but rather by using the analogy of a measurable surface, he is guiding the reader to a reality which is infinite and without limit. Here then is something of the meaning of the text as I see it: Seeing that you have stretched forth that which is before you with a greater desire, and you never experience complete satisfaction in your progress, nor are you aware of any limit to the good, as your yearning goes out to ever more and more — here is a place with me that is so vast that he who runs in it will never be able to reach the end of his course. And yet, from another point of view, this course has its stability; for God says: *I will set thee on the rock* (Ex 34.22). But here we have a very great paradox: motion and stability are the same. For usually speaking, one who is rising is not standing still, and the man who is standing still is not rising. But here he arises precisely because he is stationary. This means that a man advances farther on the path of perfection precisely insofar as he remains fixed and immovable in good. It is impossible for a man to soar towards the heights of virtue if he tends to slip and fall in the ways of the spirit and is not firmly balanced in virtue, but is "tossed to and fro, and carried about," as the Apostle tells us (Eph 4.14), fluctuating and uncertain in his ideas of reality. It is like men who try to to climb through sand. It does not matter whether they take big strides or not; they waste their effort. For their feet constantly slip to the bottom with the sand, and so, despite all their energy, they make no progress whatsover. But if, in the words of the Psalmist (Ps 39.3), a man drags his feet from the mire of the pit and sets them firmly upon the rock (and the rock is Christ, who is all perfection), the more steadfast and unshakable he becomes in good, according to the counsel of Paul, so much the more quickly will he accomplish his course. His very stability becomes a wing in his flight towards heaven; his heart becomes winged because of his stability in good."[79]

It might look quite as an antinomy, this combination of motion and stability in the pursuit of the mystical and ascetic experience and the attainment of perfection. But precisely this motion towards the higher steps and stages of the spiritual life and the stability at the same time on the premises of the true Christian life and the absolute devotion in good make possible our progress towards God. Moving always further and constantly longing for God, these are the two main aspects of the ascetic life. Or, as Gregory puts it more succinctly inspired from Moses' life: "This is the reason why we say that the great Moses, moving for ever forwards, did not stop in his upward climb. He set no limit to his rise to the stars. But once he had put his foot upon the ladder on which the Lord had leaned (Gen 28.13), as Jacob tells us, he constantly kept moving to the next step; and he continued to go ever higher because he always found another step that lay beyond the highest one that he had reached. . . What Moses was experiencing, I think, was a longing constantly being intensified by his hope at the Transcendent, arising from the beauty which he had already glimpsed; and this hope constantly inflamed his desire to see what was hidden because of all that he had attained at each stage."[80]

But, as we have already repeatedly said, this uphill or steep road, this constant ascent towards the divine summit combined with inner balance, with concrete spiritual stability, is a more than strenuous and exhaustive struggle; it is an awesome burden which man cannot carry by himself alone. Gregory, well aware of the Orthodox doctrine of the free will and feeling completely detached and liberated from the Pelagian and Eunomian anthropocentricism, recognizes τὴν θείαν συνεργίαν, that is the divine cooperation with man's moral effort.[81] So the Lord offers help and protection and guidance to man's lifelong spiritual endeavor. Or, as he puts it himself: "Thus far has the soul now progressed, protected by the right hand of the Lord according to the promise of the text (Exod 35.22). The hand of the Lord would refer to his creative power over all things. Indeed, the Only-begotten, by whom all things were made, is himself the place for those who run; he is, according to his own words, the very way of the course, as well as the rock for those who are well grounded, and the mansion for those who take their rest. At this point the soul will hear his call and will take its place behind him; it will follow the Lord God according to the precept of the Law (Deut 13.4). This is the call that the great David understood, when he said to him "that dwelleth in the aid of the most high" (Ps 90.1), that "he will overshadow thee with his shoulders" (Ps 90.4); for this is the same as following God, for the shoulders are at the back. Similarly he cries out, speaking of himself: "My soul hath stuck close to thee: thy right hand hath received me" (Ps 62.9). You see how the psalms support our text. For David here says that God's right hand received him who clings to him; so too, in our text, the Lord's hand covers Moses who awaits the divine call within the rock and asks to follow him."[82]

But Gregory proceeds still further in his allegorical study and interpretation of the biblical text. What is the meaning — Saint Gregory asks — of God's promise that Moses would see only his back on Mount Sinai? No serious student of the biblical text will take this promise in its literal sense. "For we may not speak of front and back save of things which have dimension. But the dimensions of every body are limited. Hence if you imagine that God has dimension, you cannot avoid giving him a corporeal nature. Further, all bodies are composites; and composites exist by means of the union of their various parts. Hence a composite cannot be incorruptible. And what is corruptible cannot be eternal, since corruption is simply the separation of the parts of the composite. If then we were to take the text about God's back literally, we would be logically forced into an absurd conclusion. Front and back are said of dimension; dimension applies only to bodies; and bodies, like all composites, are essentially corruptible. What is corruptible cannot be eternal. Thus if you were completely dependent on the literal meaning, you would be logically forced to admit corruption in God. Yet God is incorporeal and incorruptible."[83]

It is evident, therefore, that the entire context of the sacred text forced us to seek another interpretation, another meaning, which naturally must be applicable to the life of the ascetic. There is again here the constant parallel between the life of Moses and the life of the ascetic. They both seek to see God, they both have to suffer for it, they both must remain fixed and immovable in their ultimate goal. And as Moses needed the help and guidance of the Lord, so much the same for the ascetic. So when Moses can look only at the back of the Lord, this means that he must follow him with absolute trust and dedication watching only the back of his guide and not in any other direction. This is the example every true ascetic must follow. "Moses sought to seek God," Saint Gregory writes, "and this is the instruction he receives on how he is to see him: seeing God means following him wherever he might lead. And God's passing refers to his leading of those who follow him. Anyone who does not know the way cannot travel safely without following a guide. The guide shows him the way by walking ahead of him. And the one following will not get off the right path if he keeps constantly watching the back of his guide. On the other hand, if he moves off to one side, or tries to bring himself face to face with his guide, he will be setting out on a different path from the one which his guide is showing him. Thus the Lord says to those who are being guided: Do not face my face

(Ex 33.20), or, in other words: Do not face your guide. For then you will be going in a completely opposite direction. Good does not go in the opposite direction to good, but follows it. And that which is opposed to the good comes face to face with it. Evil looks in a different direction from virtue; but virtue does not come face to face with virtue. Hence Moses does not see God face to face, but merely looks at his back. Whoever would see him face to face would not live, as the inspired word tell us: *No man shall see* the face of the Lord *and live* (Ex 33.20). You then see how important it is to learn how to follow the Lord. For even after all those lofty ascents, those terrible and splendid visions, Moses, although he is practically at the end of his life, is hardly judged worthy of the grace, he who has learnt to walk behind his Lord. But following God in this way he no longer encounters the obstacles of sin."[84]

But where did the Lord lead Moses? Where does the Lord lead the ascetic man? What is the ultimate goal of this constant ascent and this need for moral stability? Of course, they do lead towards perfection; but is perfection in itself the summit of all the human efforts, or, to be more precise, is perfection the only fruit of the divine and human synergy in the realm of redemption?

We have already pointed to the trilogy of the ascetic life: ascent, virtue and contemplation.[85] Contemplation or θεωρία is in reality the divine reward for this synergy. It is the vision of the heavenly Tabernacle,[86] "the mysteries of Paradise,"[87] the road and the progress of he soul towards the vision of the Transcendent Being, the inner conviction that "the more it approaches this vision, [and] so much the more does it see that the divine nature is invisible."[88]

One should not expect a systematic and scholarly definition of θεωρία by Gregory of Nyssa. He writes his *Life of Moses* not as a secular philosopher but as a man of profound religious experience. His aim was no other than to present to his ascetic readers the road to spiritual perfection and the way which leads to the Divine. Jaeger has pointed out that "Gregory felt that the idea of the ascetic life was a parallel and in many ways a direct continuation of that noble tradition of the *via contemplativa* begun by the philosophers of ancient Greece. That he saw his own ideals in this perspective is obvious from the language he uses in his ascetic treatises. He makes frequent and conscious use of the terms of the philosophic tradition."[89]

We have spoken already at the first part of the present work about the relation of Gregory's thought with Greek philosopy and culture. However, in order to understand the concept of θεωρία in Gregory of Nyssa, one should not try to find a parallel in the *via contemplativa* of the Greek philosophers. For Gregory, θεωρία is not simply the Platonic condition of the mind; neither is it the Aristotelian definition of the philosopher's life. For him. θεωρία springs from the religious and historical experience of the Church and has biblical roots (hence the life of Moses as a prototype of the Christian contemplation), and aims at the salvation of the whole man in Christ and through Christ. This is why the θεωρία of Gregory of Nyssa and of he whole patristic tradition should be looked at not as an abstract, static, speculative condition of the human intellect, or of the human soul, but through the scope of the full participation of the Christian in the sacramental life of the Church. This is why Saint Gregory does not fail to stress more than emphatically in his *Life of Moses,* a highly contemplative book, the real meaning and the ultimate purpose of the sacraments of baptism and eucharist.

It has been maintained that in Gregory of Nyssa we can distinguish three important stages or rather three "ways" in man's mystical ascent towards God.[90] As Moses proceeded from the light to the cloud and then to the divine darkness of Mount Sinai, so man through illumination, contemplation and mystical participation with God can reach his ultimate goal in uniting himself with God.[91] One should not expect to find in *Life of Moses* a systematic and distinctive description of three exactly separated stages of this mystical ascent. We have already said that no systematic difinition of the mystical life is offered by the Fathers of the Church. It is clear, however, that a man who really wants to reach the summit of the mystical experience in being with God, needs first, to follow and endless road, a road without any stop towards his ultimate goal; secondly, he must be inspired by a profound desire and longing for God; and thirdly, he must achieve a complete an absolute purity of his whole self.

Thus for Gregory of Nyssa, no obstacle would interrupt the motion of the soul upwards. The soul, free from the downward motion of the heavy sinful bodies, will swiftly move upwards, released from the sensuous and earthly attachments, soaring from the world below, up towards the heavens.[92] The soul will keep "rising higher, and higher, stretching with its desire for heavenly things to those that are before (Phil 3.13), as the Apostle tells us, and thus it will always continue to soar even higher."[93] This motion upwards is ceaseless, "ἄπαυστον ποιεῖται τὴν ἐπὶ τὸ ἄνω φοράν . . . or "πάντοτε πρὸς τὴν πτῆσιν ποιήσεται . . ."[94] So, " . . . because of what it has already attained, the soul does not wish to abandon the heights that lie beyond it. And thus the soul moves ceaselessly upwards, always reviving its tension for its onward flight by means of the progress it has already realized. Indeed, it is only spiritual activity that nourishes its force by exercise; it does not slacken its tension by action but rather increases it."[95]

This constant motion upwards should be kindled by the deepest desire and longing for God. Saint Gregory speaks of ἐρωτικὴν διάθεσιν,[96] σφοδρὸν ἐραστὴν τοῦ κάλλους, ἐκκαίουσαν ἐπιθυμίαν,[97] or τὸ μηδέποτε τῆς ἐπιθυμίας κόρον εὑρεῖν . . .[98] It is an intensified kind of love inflamed by the inner desire to see God, always dissatified, always thirsty, always begging God to give him more; " . . . he asks God to show himself to him, not now by way of analogy, but as he is in himself."[99] Look at Moses, Saint Gregory reminds to us. God granted that his desire to see God would be fulfilled. But he did not promise that this desire would ever cease or be fully satisfied; " . . . for the true vision of God ("τοῦ ἀηθῶς ἰδεῖν τὸν Θεόν") consists rather in this: that the soul that looks up to God never ceases to desire him . . . Thus it is that Moses' desire is filled by the very fact that it remains unfulfilled."[100]

This unfulfilled longing of seeing God must have as a constant companion purity of heart and body . . . "The person who wants to consecrate himself to God must bring his body to the altar and become a living sacrifice, by offering his life in *a reasonable service* (Rom 12.1); he must not weigh down his soul with the thick and heavy garment of a sensuous life, but he must make all the actions of his life as thin as a spider's web by the purity of his conduct . . . "[101] "Καθαρότης τῆς ζωῆς" or "τὸ λαμπρὸν καὶ καθαρὸν τοῦ βίου"[102] is indispensable for the mystical ascent of the soul, for the contemplation of God. Saint Gregory explains this prerequisite in the most convincing way: "The way," he writes, "that leads to this knowledge [of God] is purity — a purity that is not merely bodily, achieved by ritual washings, but one that touches all our clothing, for they must be rinsed of every stain in the water. And this means that the man who would approach the contemplation of truth must cleanse himself and remove all impurity from both soul and body, so as to be completely stainless and pure in both. Our exterior behavior must correspond to the inner state of our soul, that we might be pure for him who sees the interior. Hence by divine command, before climbing the mountain we must wash our garments; and here clothing is a symbol for the external virtuousness of our lives. No one could hold that a visible spot on our clothing would be an obstacle in our ascent towards God; rather, I think that clothing here aptly refers to the external actions of our lives."[103]

Then when we become "superior to all sense perception" or when we wash "from our minds any opinion based on sense perception," when purify our conduct "of all sensuous or animal behavior," then we may dare "to attempt the mountain," "to approach the knowledge of he mysteries . . . "[104] and "rise (as Moses) even further towards the heights of spiritual reality."[105]

But what is this "spiritual reality"? We have already spoken of this spiritual reality as the divine illumination, as the spiritual knowledge of God; it is "ἡ πρώτη θεοφάνεια," "τῆς εὐσεβείας ἡ γνῶσις,"[106] "ἡ ἄρρητος φωταγωγία,"[107] "ἡ ἀπόρρητος θεογνωσία,"[108] "ἡ δόξα τοῦ Θεοῦ."[109] We have spoken also of "contemplation" or "θεωρία" as the third stage of this spiritual reality and of "γνόφος" as the third stage towards God. At this final stage we can say that we may see God. But what does the expression, "ἰδεῖν τὸν Θεόν,"[110] really mean? It is more than interesting that Saint Gregory uses here two words completely contrary and opposite to each other: He speaks of "λαμπρὸς γνόφος,"[111] "the luminous darkness." This seeming contradiction of terminology brings up now a basic truth of the mystical life: that although we must strive constantly towards God, we must be ready to submit ourselves to the awareness of the incomprehensibility of God. To enter this "luminous dearkness" means that we enter the "Holy of Holies" or the "heavenly Tabernacle." It is place which is forbidden to the multitude and it is inacccessible and incomprehensible to the majority: "ἀληθῶς γὰρ ἅγιόν τι χρῆμά ἐστι καὶ ἁγίων ἅγιον καὶ τοῖς πολλοῖς ἄληπτόν τε καὶ ἀπρόσιτον ἡ τῶν ὄντων ἀλήθεια . . . " Saint Gregory, with absolute humility, repeatedly reminds his readers that "we must not search after a knowledge of things which are beyond our comprehension; rather we must believe that what we seek really exists even though it is not obvious to the eyes of all, but remains hidden in the secret recesses of the spirit."[113] Thus Saint Gregory is here in full accord with the patristic tradition of the Church. He claims, therefore, that the divinity "transcends all knowledge,"[114] the "true Being" is "true Life" and "cannot be known by us,"[115] or that "the divine is by its very nature infinite and cannot be circumscribed by any definite term . . . "[116] In splendid and pertinent Greek terminology, Saint Gregory speaks of "τὸ τῆς θείας φύσεως ἀθεώρητον" and that when Moses increased in knowledge, then he entered in the darkness of seeing God, that is, he then realized that to see God means to become aware that the divine is superior of any knowledge and comprehension: "Ὅτε οὖν μείζων ἐγένετο κατὰ τὴν γνῶσιν ὁ Μωϋσῆς, τότε ὁμολογεῖ ἐν γνόφῳ τὸν Θεὸν ἰδεῖν, τουτέστι τότε γνῶναι ὅτι ἐκεῖνό ἐστι τῇ φύσει τὸ θεῖον, ὃ πάσης γνώσεώς τε καὶ καταλήψεώς ἐστιν ἀνώτερον . . . "[117]

It seems more than appropriate to quote here the whole paragraph in which the great Cappadocian Father explains the process which leads to the luminous darkness of the incomprehensibility of God: "But what now is the meaning of Moses' entry into the darkness and of the vision of God that he enjoyed in it? The present text (Ex 24.15) would seem to be somewhat contradictory to the divine apparition he has seen before. There he saw God in the light, whereas here he sees him in the darkness. But we should not therefore think that this contradicts the entire sequence of spiritual lessons which we have been considering. For the sacred text is here teaching us that spiritual knowledge first occurs as an illumination in those who experience it. Indeed, all that is opposed to piety is conceived of as darkness; to shun the darkness is to share in the light. But as the soul makes progress, and by a greater and more perfect concentration comes to appreciate what the knowledge of truth is, the more it approaches this vision, and so much the more does it see that the divine nature is invisible. It thus leaves all surface appearances, not only those that can be grasped by the senses but also those which the mind itself seems to see, and it keeps on going deeper until by the operation of the spirit it penetrates the invisible and incomprehensible, and it is there that it sees God. The true vision and the true knowledge of what we seek consists precisely in not seeing, in an awareness that our goal transcends all knowledge and is everywhere cut off from us by the darkness of incomprehensibility ("'καταλιπὼν γὰρ πᾶν τὸ φαινόμενον οὐ μόνον ὅσα καταλαμβάνει ἡ αἴσθησις ἀλλὰ καὶ ὅσα ἡ διάνοια δοκεῖ βλέπειν, ἀεὶ πρὸς τὸ ἐνδότερον ἵεται ἕως ἂν διαδυῇ καὶ τῇ πολυπραγματοσύνῃ τῆς διανοίας πρὸς τὸ ἀθέατόν τε καὶ ἀκατάληπτον κἀκεῖ τὸν Θεὸν ᾿ίδῃ. Ἐν τούτῳ γὰρ ἡ ἀληθής ἐστιν εἴδησις τοῦ ζητουμένου καὶ ἐν τούτῳ τὸ ἰδεῖν ἐν τῷ μὴ ἰδεῖν, ὅτι ὑπέρκειται πάσης εἰδήσεως τὸ ζητούμενον οἷόν τινι γνόφῳ τῇ ἀκαταληψίᾳ πανταχόθεν διειλημμένον''). Thus that profound evangelist, John, who penetrated into this luminous darkness (λαμπρῷ γνόφῳ), tells that "no man hath seen God at any time" (Jn 11.18), teaching us by this negation that no man — indeed, no created intellect — can attain a knowledge of God ("ἀλλὰ καὶ πάσῃ τῇ νοητῇ φύσει τῆς θείας οὐσίας τὴν γνῶσιν ἀνέφικτον εἶναι τῇ ἀποφάσει ταύτῃ διοριζόμενος'').[118]

Unfortunately, the English translation cannot fully render the power and the mystical insight of the original Greek text. Indeed, no created intellect can ever reach the divine "ousia"; Saint Gregory is axiomatic on that. Man, however, can live with God a life of light and incorruption, being always in the image of the incorruptible and immutable Archetype.[119]

Then he becomes a real servant of God (οἰκέτης τοῦ Θεοῦ) or more precisely a friend of God (φίλος τοῦ Θεοῦ), which is the most honorable and blessed goal of the life of perfection.[120]

This is in substance the message which Saint Gregory of Nyssa brings

forth in his *Life of Moses*. Now, of course, the question which might arise
is this: In what respect and what dimension does this message have any
relevance to our contemporary world and to our "modern" man? Or
how can the man of our technocratic society today live a life of contemplation, a life of spiritual perfection? For the secular man of today the answer
cannot be easy and direct.

And yet we must not fail here to stress the fact that both Moses and
Saint Gregory of Nyssa were "modern" men in the proper sense of the
word. They fully lived their time, they fully participated in the events
of their history-making epochs, they lived and fought as men of action,
as men of the world and society. They were both married, they were both
leaders of people, they both faced all the temptations and disillusions
of life. However, they both met squarely all the problems of life and both
displayed a rare combination of activism and contemplation. Thus they
taught posterity that a life of action and a life of contemplation are not
exclusive to each other. They have shown that the life which leads to
perfection is a full life, a life of action which demands work, sacrifice
and sweat. Above all, however, they have shown that beyond any involvement in this world, there lies the life of faith, the life of contemplation
which gives man an impetus, so that he may become again a "friend
of God," as he was at the day of his creation.

NOTES

[1]Werner Jaeger, *Two Rediscovered Works of Ancient Christian Literature:
Gregory of Nyssa and Macarius* (Leiden, 1954), p. 138.

[2]*De Instituto Christiano*, ed. by W. Jaeger in his *Gregorii Nysseni Opera
Ascetica* (Leiden, 1952), pp. 41, 64, 66, 79.

[3]Ibid p. 83.

[4]Jaeger, *Two Rediscovered Works*, p. 20.

[5]*De Vita Moysis*, ed. by H. Musurillo (Leiden, 1964), p. 83. See also *From Glory
to Glory*, Texts from Gregory of Nyssa's Mystical Writings, ed. by Jean Danielou
and H. Musurillo (New York, 1961), p. 97.

[6]*De Vita Moysis*, ed. W. Jaeger, p. 91 and Danielou, *Glory*, p. 132.

[7]*De Vita Moysis*, p. 118: "πέτρα δὲ ἐστιν ὁ Χριστός, ἡ παντελὴς ἀρετή" and
Danielou, *Glory* p. 149.

[8]*De Vita Moysis*, 121: "ὁρᾷς ὅσον ἐστὶ τὸ μαθεῖν, ἀκολουθῆσαι Θεῶ" Danielou
and H. Musurillo, *Glory*p. 152.

[9]*De Vita Moysis*, p. 121: "Οὐκοῦν διδάσκεται νῦν ὁ Μωϋσῆς, ὁ ἰδεῖν τὸν Θεὸν
σπεύδων, πῶς ἔστιν ἰδεῖν τὸν Θεόν, ὅτι τὸ ἀκολουθεῖν τῷ Θεῷ καθ' ὅπερ ἄν
καθοδηγῇται, τοῦτο βλέπειν ἐστὶ τὸ Θεόν." Danielou and Musurillo, *Glory*, p. 151.

[10]*De Vita Moysis*, p. 86: "Τὶ δὲ βούλεται τὸ ἐντὸς τὸν Μωϋσέα καὶ οὕτως ἐν
αὐτῷ τὸν Θεὸν ἰδεῖν"; Ibid, p. 118.

[11]Harold Frederick Cherniss, *The Platonism of Gregory of Nyssa,* University of California Publications in Classical Philology, vol. 11 (1930), pp. 1-92.

[12]Ibid. p. 61.

[13]Ibid. pp. 63-64.

[14]Ibid. pp. 35 and 43. See also: *De Vita Moysis,* p. 40.

[15]H. Cherniss, *Platonism,* p. 11.

[16]*De Vita Moysis,* p. 43: "ἡ ἀλλοφύλων ὁμόζυγος." See also, Harry A. Wolfson, *The Philosophy of the Church Fathers* (Cambridge, Mass., 1956), p. 98.

[17]*De Vita Moysis,* p. 36.

[18]Ibid. p. 35: "Κιβωτὸς δ' ἂν εἴν ἐκ διαφόρων σανίδων συμπεπηγυῖα παίδευσις, ἡ ἄνω τῶν κυμάτων τὸν δι' αὐτῆς ἐπιφερόμενον τοῦ βίου ἀνέχουσα . . . " Gregory most of the time makes the due distinction between philosophy as such and encyclopaedic secular learning. The latter of course is of lower grade; both, however, are equally sterile and fruitless: ἄγονοι and στεῖραι. Ibid. pp. 36-36.

[19]Ibid.

[20]Jaeger, *Two Rediscovered Works,* p. 137.

[21]*De Vita Moysis,* p. 43: "ἔστι γάρ τι καὶ τῆς ἔξω παιδεύσεως πρὸς συζυγίαν ἡμῶν εἰς τεκνοποιΐαν ἀρετῆς οὐκ ἀπόβλητον. Καὶ γὰρ ἡ ἠθική τε καὶ φυσικὴ φιλοσοφία γένοιτο ἄν ποτε τῷ ὑψηλοτέρῳ βίῳ σύζηγός τε καὶ φίλη καὶ κοινωνὸς τῆς ζωῆς, μόνον εἰς τὰ ἐκ ταύτης κυήματα μηδὲν ἐπάγοιτο τοῦ ἀλλοφύλου μιάσματος.». See also J. Quasten, *Patrology,* vol. 3 (Westminster, Md., 1960), p. 284.

[22]*De Vita Moysis,* p. 2: ". . . τῇ πολιᾷ ταύτῃ νεότητος σωφροσύνης ἐπίταγμα δέχεσθαι".

[23]Gregory wrote his *De Vita Moysis* about the year 390. He was then about sixty years of age and as far as we can know he did not live beyond the middle of he 390ᵃs.

[24]Jaeger, *Two Rediscovered Works,* p. 136.

[25]*De Vita Moysis,* p. 44.

[26]Ibid. p. 68.

[27]Jean Danielou, *Platonism et Theologie Mystique, Essai sur la doctrine spirituelle de saint Gregoire de Nysse* (Paris, 1944); Danielou and Musurillo, *Glory.* For complete bibliography on the subject see above as well as Quasten, *Patrology,* Vol. 3, pp. 254ff.

[28]*De Vita Moysis,* pp. 68-69.

[29]Ibid. pp. 56, 57, 60, 61, 62, 70, 72, 73, 74, 75, 76, 78, 80, 103, 107. See slso pp. 86. 133, 134, 135, 136, 141, 144.

[30]Ibid. pp. 128-9.

[31]Ibid. p. 72: " . . . παιδεύει διὰ τούτων ἡ ἱστορία. . . and p. 80: "διὸ μόνην τὴν πρὸς τὸ κρεῖττον κατορθουμένην παρασκευὴν νομοθετεῖ τοῖς ἀνθρώποις ἱστορία . . .

[32]Ibid. pp. 128-129, 133, 135 ff.

[33]J. Danielou, *Platonism et Theologie Mystique,* pp. 99-110. For the relation of Greek paideia and Christianity see also John P. Cavarnos, "Gregory of Nyssa on the Nature of the soul," in *The Greek Orthodox Theological Review* 1 (1955) 134.

[34]*De Vita Moysis,* p. 108.

[35]Ibid. pp. 107-09.

[36]Ibid. p. 109.

[37]Ibid. p. 39.

[38]Ibid. p. 41.

[39]Ibid. p. 77 and Danielou, *Glory*, p. 96.

[40]*De Vita Moysis*, pp. 118, 119.

[41]Ibid, pp. 42, 83, 127-128.

[42]Ibid. pp. 71-72.

[43]Ibid. p. 70.

[44]Ibid. p. 73 and Danielou, *Glory*, p. 92.

[45]*De Vita Moysis*, p. 125.

[46]Ibid. p. 75. See also: Danielou, *Glory*, pp. 94-95.

[47]Georges Florovsky, The Predicament of Christian Historian," in *Religion and Culture*, Essays in honor of Paul Tillich, edited by Walter Leibrecht (New York, 1959), p. 146.

[48]*De Vita Moysis*, pp. 91-2 and Danielou, *Glory*, p. 132.

[49]*De Vita Moysis*, p. 120 and Danielou, *Glory*, p. 150.

[50]"'Ἀρχηγὸς τῆς σωτηρίας ἡμῶν". See in his *Catechetical Oration*, ed. by J. H. Srawley (Cambridge, 1956), p. 132.

[51]*Commentary on the Canticle*, Danielou, *Glory*, p. 170.

[52]*De Vita Moysis*, p. 41.

[53]Ibid. p. 127: "ὁ δὲ ἀληθὴς ὄφις ἡ ἁμαρτία ἐστί, καὶ ὁ πρὸς τὴν ἁμαρτίαν αὐτομολήσας τὴν τοῦ ὄφεως ὑποδύεται φύσιν. Ἐλευθεροῦται οὖν τῆς ἁμαρτίας ὁ ἄνθρβπος διὰ τοῦ ὑπελθόντος τὸ τῆς ἁμαρτίας εἶδος καὶ γενομένου καθ' ἡμᾶς τοὺς πρὸς τὸ εἶδος μεταστραφέντας τοῦ ὄφεως . . . ".

[54]Ibid. p. 73.

[55]Ibid. 72.

[56]Ibid. p. 72 and Danielou, *Glory*, pp. 92-93.

[57]*De Vita Moysis*, pp. 67.: "Οὕτως ἐκβάλλει τῆς Αἰγύπτου ὁ Μωϋσεῖ κατ' ἴχνος ἐπόμενος τῷ τρόπῳ τούτῳ τῆς Αἰγυπτίας τυραννίδος ἐλευθεροῖ πάντας ὧν ἂν ὁ λόγος καθίκηται . . ." Danielou, *Glory*, pp. 90-93.

[58]*De Virginitate, in Gregorii Nysseni Opera Ascetica*, edited by W. Jaeger, John Cavarnos and Virginia W. Callahan (Leiden, 1952), p. 274. See also: A Select Library of Nicene and Post-Nicene Fathers of the Christian Church (Grand Rapids, Mich., 1954), 5, p. 350.

[59]Ibid. pp. 350-51 and *De Virginitate*, 276-77, *De Vita Moysis*, pp. 77 and 82.

[60]Ibid. p. 113.

[61]Ibid, pp. 60 and 68. For a thorough analysis and discussion on the concept of freedom in Saint Gregory of Nyssa see: Jérome Gaitr, *La conception de la Liberté chez Grégoire de Nysse* (Paris, 1953), especially in pp. 40 ff.

[62]*De Vita Moysis*, pp. 74-75 and Danielou, *Glory*, p. 94.

[63]*De Vita Moysis*, pp. 88, 99, 102.

[64]Ibid. pp. 131-33.

[65]Ibid. pp. 3-4 and J. Danielou, *Glory*, p. 81.

[66]*De Vita Moysis*, p. 4 and J. Danielou, *Glory*, p. 82.

[67]*De Perfectione*, ed. by W. Jaeger, in *Gregorii Nysseni Opera Ascetica* (Leiden, 1952), p. 214 and Danielou, *Glory*, p. 84.

[68]*De Vita Moysis*, p. 139.

[69]Ibid. pp. 112-13.

[70]Ibid. pp. 118.

[71]Ibid. pp. 116.

[72]Ibid. p. 43.

[73]Ibid. p. 116.

[74]Ibid. P. 86.

[75]Ibid. p. 142.

[76]Ibid. p. 82.

[77]Ibid. p. 117. See also Danielou, *Glory* p. 148.

[78]*De Vita Moysis*, p. 117 and Danielou, *Glory*, p. 148.

[79]*De Vita Moysis*, pp. 117-18 and Danielou, *Glory*, pp. 148-150.

[80]Ibid. pp. 113-14 and Danielou, *Glory*, pp. 144-146.

[81]W. Jaeger, *Two Rediscovered Works* pp. 90 ff. where one can find a pertinent discussion of the doctrine of Divine Synergy in Saint Gregory of Nyssa.

[82]*De Vita Moysis*, p. 120 and Danielou, *Glory*, pp. 150-51.

[83]*De Vita Moysis*, pp. 110-11Q » . . .τὸ γὰρ ἐμπρόσθιόν τε καὶ ὀπίσθιον ἐν σχήματι πάντως, τὸ δὲ σχῆμα ἐν σώματι. Τοῦτο δὲ διαλυτὸν κατὰ τὴν ἰδίαν φύσιν ἐστι. Διαλυτὸν γὰρ ἄπαν τὸ σύνθετον. Τὸ δὲ λυόμενον ἄφθαρτον εἶναι οὐ δύναται. Ἄρα ὁ τᾷ γράμματι δουλεύων φθορὰν διὰ τῆς ἀκολουθίας τῶν νοημάτων περὶ τὸ θεῖον ἐννοήσειεν. Ἀλλὰ μὴ ῎αφθαρτος ὁ Θεὸς καὶ ἀσώματος.» See also, Danielou, *Glory*, p. 143.

[84]*De Vita Moysis*, pp. 121-22 and Danielou, *Glory*, pp. 151-52.

[85]See p. 12.

[86]*De Vita Moysis*, p. 97 and Danielou, *Glory*, pp. 136-38.

[87]*De Vita Moysis*, p. 93.

[88]Ibid. pp. 83 and 86 ff. and Danielou, *Glory*, pp. 97 and 118.

[89]Jaeger, *Two Rediscovered Works*, pp. 20-21.

[90]Moutsoula, "'Η Σάρκωσις τοῦ Λόγου καὶ ἡ θέωσις τοῦ 'ανθρώπου κατὰ τὴν διδασκαλίαν Γρηγορίου τοῦ Νύσσης (Athens, 1965), p. 201.

[91]Ibid.

[92]*De Vita Moysis*, p. 112 and J. Danielou, *From Glory to Glory*, p. 144. For the nature of he soul in Gregory of Nyssa see John P. Cavarnos, "Gregory of Nyssa on the Nature of the Soul," in the *Greek Orthodox Theological Review*, (March, 1955) 133 ff.

[93]*De Vita Moysis*, p. 112.

[94]Ibid.

[95]Ibid. pp. 112-13 and Danielou, *From Glory to Glory*, 144.

[96]*De Vita Moysis*, p. 114.

[97]Ibid.

[98]Ibid. 116.

[99]Ibid. pp. 113-14 and Danielou, *From Glory to Glory*, p. 145.

[100]*De Vita Moysis, and Danielou, From Glory to Glory*, pp. 146-47

[101]*De Vita Moysis*, pp. 98-99 and Danielou, *From Glory to Glory*, p. 138.

[102]*De Vita Moysis*, pp. 98 and 101 and Danielou, *From Glory to Glory*, p. 140.

[103]*De Vita Moysis*, p. 83 and Danielou, *From Glory to Glory*, p. 97.

[104]*De Vita Mousis*, p. 84 and Danielou, *From Glory to Glory*, p. 98.

[105]*De Vita Moysis*, p. 97 Danielou, *From Glory to Glory*, pp. 137-38.

[106] *De Vita Moysis*, p. 86 and Danielou, *From Glory to Glory*, p. 118.

[107]*De Vita Moysis*, pp. 39 and 60.

[108]Ibid. 82.

[109]Ibid. pp. 89, 109, 110 and 113.

[110]Ibid. p. 87.

[111]Ibid.

[112]Ibid. p. 97. See also Danielou, *From Glory to Glory*, 137.

[113]Ibid.

[114]*De Vita Moysis*, p. 115 and Danielou, *From Glory to Glory p. 146*.

[115]*Ibid.*

[116]*De Vita Moysis*, p. 115 and Danielou, *Glory to Glory*, p. 147.

[117]*De Vita Moysis*, 87.

[118]*De Vita Moysis*, pp. 86-87 and Danielou, *Glory to Glory*, p. 118.

[119]*De Vita Moysis*, 143.

[120]Ibid. pp.144-45.

Saint John Chrysostom:
On Materialism and Christian Virtue

Saint John Chrysostom is a great Father and preacher of the Church. He was a profound exponent of Scriptures, the most eloquent preacher of all time. This earnest and sincere teacher of Christian morals was an adamant and most fearless believer in our Savior, the Lord Jesus Christ. It is, indeed, with great humility and deep fear of God, that I come to you today to speak about this holy man, whose life has been totally immersed in the Spirit of God, completely dedicated to the Christian Church, wholeheartedly devoted to a true transfiguration of this world and to the ultimate goal of human existence — to victory, joy, and theosis.

John Chrysostom is a hero in the true sense of the term; thus, he is able to inspire us with his intellectual genius, as well as his superb moral character, his strong boldness of purpose, and the burning flame of his true piety. His glowing personality has inspired generation upon generation, and his genuine ecclesiastical spirit (*phronema*) has indeed become the example *par excellance* to follow for true churchmen, priests, and theologians.

I agree with Philip Schaff who states that Saint John Chrysostom excelled in "the fulness of Scripture knowledge, the intense earnestness, the fruitfulness of illustration and application, the variation of topics, the command of language, the elegance and rhythmic flow of his Greek style, the dramatic vivacity, the quickness and ingenuity of his turns, and the magnetism of sympathy with his hearers . . . "[1]

But beyond this eloquent description of Saint John Chrysostom's virtues, I am compelled to say that Saint John Chrysostom was great because
he was both human and holy. He was "a man of his time and for all
times";[2] a man of the world, but he overcame the world and became the
harp, the instrument, the mouth — the fervent witness of the Holy Spirit.

I can imagine what he would have said if he were alive today. I can
see how his fierce tongue, his sparkling eyes, his piercing voice, and his
angry pen would have protested upon seeing the same materialistic spirit
of today, as well as the same secular approach towards life, the same
yearning for material success, and the same idolatrous admiration given
to greed, self-interest, and self-centeredness.

A few weeks ago, in a prestigious newspaper, a journalist of national
fame wrote a very strange article under the title "An Ode to Greed."
The subtitle was "Time for Delisting from the 'Seven Deadly Sins.' "[3]
The seven deadly sins listed by Saint Gregory the Great, bishop of Rome,
in the year 600 were anger, envy, lust, gluttony, pride, envy, and greed.
The newspaperman strongly suggests that the last one should be removed
from the famous list. Our author writes that greed is hunger for more,
"but only a hearty welcome to the demands of the truly greedy can in-
sure ample supply for truly needy."[4] Finally, the same author appears
to suggest that pride should also be removed from the old-fashioned list
of the seven "deadly sins." This is the spirit of the world today. It is
comprised of greed, success, and "the profit motive." This is the "best
engine of betterment to man."[5] The conclusion is that without greed
there is no generosity.[6]

The biblical and patristic approach is completely different. Worldly
things are alien to the basic Christian precepts of godliness, virtue, and
piety. The Lord himself taught us that he "is not of this world" (Jn 8.23,
17.14), that there is another "prince of this world" (Jn 12.31), that he
himself "has conquered the world" (Jn 16.33), and "that his kingdom
does not belong to this world" (Jn 18.36). Saint Paul speaks repeatedly
about "the spirit" or the "wisdom" of this world (1 Cor 2.12, 3.19). The
exhortation of Saint John the Evangelist is so pertinent: "Do not love
the world or the things in the world. If anyone loves the world, love for
the Father is not in him. For all that is in the world, the lust of the flesh
and the lust of the eyes and the glamour of life, is not of the Father
but is of this world. And the world and the lust of it passes away, but
he who does the will of God abides forever" (1 Jn 2.15-17). Also in agreement with this teaching is the extremely well-known parable of our Lord
concerning the rich man and poor Lazaros as recorded by Saint Luke
(16.19-31). Here, we are told of all "the good things" of this world

which fell upon the rich man and all the "bad things" which fell upon poor Lazaros, as well as the consequences of their behavior and actions.

Thus, it is very clear that in the New Testament a line is drawn between the spirit and riches of this world and the spirit of Christ, the spirit of truth (Rom 8.19), and the "Spirit of God" (1 Cor 7.40).

Saint John Chrysostom possessed a sharp, analytical mind, high morality, pure faith, and such stature that he could not but embrace totally and unquestionably this spirit of the Scriptures. Although he had the opportunity to enjoy all the pleasures of this world, from his youth he abandoned everything for the sake of Christ and his holy Church. We know that his commitment to monastic life and its strict rules was thorough and unfading. He wrote three long homilies against those who oppose monasticism, and he praised the sweetness and the calmness of the soul and the endless exuberance (*euphrosyne*)[7] of the monastic life. The monks are the true "Christ-bearing temples and heavenly athletes."[8] In one of his shortest yet most memorable homilies, he compared the life of a king with the life of a monk, and he came to the conclusion that the life of a monk is superior to that of a king; for whereas the king has to deal with the worldly affairs of this life day and night, the monk "decorates his life with the true worship of God and with prayers so as to live together with the angels and to talk with God himself."[9] He constantly reminds his readers that the simplicity of the monastic life guarantees health; carefree, quiet nights; and sound health to the monks.[10] "When you see," he writes, "a master of wealth dressed with luxurious clothes, decorated with gold, and brought to and fro in vehicles and in splendid and pompous processions, do not envy him. However, when you see a monk, walking by himself, humbly and meekly, quietly and peacefully, become an imitator of his philosophy, and pray that you may become like him."[11]

Chrysostom, however, also poses the question: Should all the inhabitants of the cities therefore desert them and go to live in the deserts and upon the peaks of mountains? He emphatically replies — not at all! Saint John Chrysostom is a practical man. What he really wants to convey is that worldly glory, wealth, luxury, and greed do not bring about happiness, fame, and fulfillment. It is most astonishing that in his second homily against those who oppose monasticism, he uses four examples from ancient Greece: Socrates, Plato, Diogenes and Aristides as examples of humility, wisdom, poverty, and simplicity. Early Christianity and Greek paideia and ethos are truly married in this beautiful homily of Saint John Chrysostom.

As a man of such human dimensions, Saint John Chrysostom is fully
aware of the biblical understanding of material things. The terms which
he frequently uses are *cosmos* which is the world, as well as cosmikos
which refers to worldly things and affairs. In his seventy-ninth homily
on the Gospel of Saint John, he clearly expresses his feelings about this
world or cosmos:

> Let us, then, overcome the world; let us hasten to immortality; let
> us follow after our King; let us set up a trophy for him; let us despise
> the pleasures of the world. Moreover, there is no need of toils; let
> us transfer our soul to heaven, and the whole world has been con-
> quered. If you do not desire it, it has been vanquished; if you ridicule
> it, it has been worsted.[12]

Again Saint Chrysostom speaks of the vanity and ephemeral character
of this world, as well as the transient nature of our life. He frequently
writes that "we are strangers and travelers."[13] We all live in a "strange
and foreign land"; and therefore, nothing "in this alien country" should
trouble us.[14] People, many times are like the running water "cold and
weak and inconstant"; and they are attached to the passing things of
this life, "never constant, always bearing us downhill precipitously. And
this is so, because today a man is rich; tomorrow poor. Today he appears with a herald, and purse, and chariot, and many attendants; frequently, on the following day he has taken up his abode in a prison, for-
saking to another, unwillingly, that show of grandeur."[15]

Besides the vanity and flux of voluptuous living, it also brings out all
kinds of illnesses. "It strips off the strength of the body and sweeps away
the virility of the soul." However, " . . . pain in the feet, and headaches,
and blindness, and pains in the hands, and trembling and paralysis, and
jaundice, lingering burning fevers, and many others in addition to these
. . . are not from abstinence and a life of self-denial, but have been caused by gluttony and satiety."[16] Also there are "the diseases of the soul"
as Saint John Chrysostom calls them, "greed, sloth, melancholy, laziness,
licentiousness" which spring from a luxurious lifestyle.[17]

Similarly, he proclaims the truth, which many medical doctors,
physiologists, dieticians, and nutritionists speak about today: "Abstinence,
in truth, as it is the mother of health, is also the mother of pleasure;
and repletion as it is the source and the root of diseases, is also provocative of disgust . . . Therefore, not only should we find the poor more
prudent and healthier than the rich, but even enjoying more happiness."[18] Additionally, he often speaks about the "glitter of this
world," the "love of glory," and the people who "are busy with tem-

poral affairs" who are in reality "citizens of this world" and who forget "the things of God" and "the things of heaven."[19] We must never forget that this life is like staying "in a hotel or inn" (*pandocheion*),[20] that this life is a continuous struggle, that this is a life of mourning and sorrow, of askesis, hardships, struggle, and sweat. There is little comfort in this life. Both the pleasant as well as the sorrowful things are and must be indifferent to us. Hence they go away with such speed, so that they may not influence us forever. Thus, he writes: "But the unseemly pleasures of this life in no way differ from shadows and dreams; for before the deed of sin is completed, the conditions of pleasure are extinguished; and the punishment for these have no limit. And the sweetness lasts for a little while, but the pain is everlasting. Tell me, what is there that is stable in this world? Wealth which does not last even to the evening? Or glory? For as they dash away before they stand still, even so does this glory take to flight before it has fairly reached us.[21]

Precisely because Saint John Chrysostom fully understands the temporal nature of earthly things, he spoke so strongly and so convincingly against the accumulation of wealth and the procurement of riches. He openly said that, "not to share one's resources is robbery." It is an astonishing statement, and Saint John Chrysostom knows this, but he brings all the necessary proofs and arguments from the Scriptures to prove his point. He uses three synonyms, *harpage, pleonexia,* and *aposteresis* in order to bring home his point that if one does not share with the needy, one is a thief.[22] We are all fellow-servants or σύνδουλοι, and we must share (μετεδίδειν) whatever we have with our brothers and sisters in Christ.

Moreover, Chrysostom asks the most tempting and provocative question: "But what is the meaning of 'mine' and 'not mine'? For truly, the more accurately I weigh these words, the more they seem to me to be but words . . . " "And not only in silver and gold, but also in bathing places, gardens, buildings, 'mine' and 'not mine' you will perceive to be but meaningless words. For use is common to all . . . " Besides "God generously gives all things that are much more necessary than money, such as air, water, fire, sun — all such things . . . " All equally enjoy these gifts of God. Thus "mine" and "thine," these "chilly" words which introduce innumerable wars into the world should be eliminated from the holy Church. . . . The legal proprietors of worldly things or goods, "who seem to be owners or masters (δοκοῦντες αὐτῶν εἶναι κύριοι — differ from those who are not even legally owners only by the fact that they have a greater responsibility to society."[23] He begs that those who possess worldly things not be possessed by these things; he states that the great inheritances of a few are unjust. The accumulation of wealth, most of the time, is acquired through sinful means. Saint Chrysostom has been charged with attacking the rich unjustly, but he knows better than that. In his famous homilies to Eutropios, he makes it very clear that he is against the corrupted character of the rich. He says:

> For I am continually saying that I do not attack the character of the rich man, but of the rapacious. A rich man is one thing, a rapacious man is another: an affluent man is one thing, a covetous man is another. Make clear distinctions, and do not confuse things which are diverse. Art thou a rich man? I forbid thee not. Art thou a rapacious man? I denounce thee. Hast thou property of thy own? Enjoy it. Dost thou take the property of others? I will not hold my peace. Wouldest thou stone me for this? I am ready to shed by blood: only I forbid thy sin. I heed not hatred, I heed not war: one thing only do I heed, the advancement of my hearers. The rich are my children, and the poor also are my children: the same womb has travailed with both, both are the same offspring of the same travail-pangs. If then thou fastenest reproaches on the poor man does not suffer so much loss as the rich. For no great wrong is inflicted on the poor man, seeing that in his case the injury is confined to money; but in thy case the injury touches the soul. Let him who wills cast me off, let him who wills stone me: for plots of enemies are the pledges to me of crowns of victory, and the number of my rewards will be as the number of my wounds.[24]

Saint John Chrysostom is ready to reply to the contemporary advocates of Social Darwinism who say that the poor are themselves the cause of their poverty because of their own wickedness and because God does not love them. He declares that this is contrary to the biblical understanding of God's love for all humankind, and it is a frivolous notion; and he further questions how they can call the rich and greedy fortunate because of their earthly belongings:

> Let us not, therefore, call them fortunate because of what they have, but miserable of what will come, because of the dreadful courtroom, because of the inexorable judgment, because of the outer darkness which awaits them . . . no one will escape God's judgment, but all who live by fraud and theft will certainly draw upon themselves that immortal and endless penalty, just like this rich man (who faced poor Lazaros).[25]

We have seven sermons of Saint John Chrysostom on Lazaros and the rich man, and one realizes immediately his profound concern about the society in which he lives. The social chasm and discrepancy in Antioch was horrendous. A few wealthy people, living in the luxurious villas of the cities, controlled most of the wealth of the city; and in Constantinople, out of the one hundred thousand Christians, fifty thousand lived below the "safety net," to use a popular social term of our time. He knew from his excellent Greek humanitarian background and his excellent biblical foundations, that injustice and the monopoly of wealth in the hands of the few are contrary to the ultimate goal and destiny of man. Was he a socialist? Indeed, Saint John Chrysostom did not support or belong to any particular political or social system. He castigated both the rich as well as the poor who violated the commandments of God. A common error of politicians of all forms and colors is that they see the Church as a so-called sociological phenomenon;[26] whereas Saint Chrysostom saw the Church as a divine organism, as the Ark of Noah, as the only place where ultimate salvation is secured for everybody regardless of social background. He saw human sufferings and human shortcomings through his sound biblical ecclesiology and eschatology. He often repeated the biblical "vanity of vanities, all is vanity." "This saying," he writes, "ought to be continually written on our walls, and garments, in the market place, and in the house, on the streets, and on the doors and entrances, and above all on the conscience of each one, and to be a perpetual theme for meditation."[27] He is interested in "faith (πίστις) and life (βίος) as found within the perimeters of the Christian Church.[28] Why? "For nothing is stronger than the Church. The Church is your hope, your salvation, your refuge . . ."[29]

In combatting materialism and greed however, Saint Chrysostom urges us to follow, within the ecclesiological setting and framework of salvation, the evangelical way of a virtuous life. He uses the beautiful Greek word ἀρετή, or virtue, which for the ancient Greeks included justice, bravery, and prudence. He incorporated it with the Christian understanding of love, humility, hope, and faith, and transformed and projected it to its eschatological vision and goal. Saint Chrysostom's theology, therefore, is not negative, but truly positive. He writes, "Let us not regard what is present, but consider what is to come. Let us examine not the outer garments, but the conscience of each person. Let us pursue the virtue and joy which come from righteous actions; and let us both, rich and poor, emulate Lazaros."[30] It has been observed by Professor Margaret Schatkin[31] that the divine Chrysostom uses the principle of Greek ethical theory to demonstrate that the Hellenic idea of virtue is realized only among Christians. Moreover, Christian virtue makes the Christian really "illustrous and distinguished."[32] He is so categorical about the practice of virtue, as he says, "for it is not possible to be saved by grace alone, but there is need of faith, and after faith, of virtue."[33] He also notes:

> But if the noun "man" furnishes such an exhortation to virtue, does not the word "faithful" give a much greater one? You are called "faithful" both because you believe in God and have as a trust from him justification, sanctity, purity of soul, filial adoption, and the kingdom of heaven. God has entrusted and given these over to your keeping; you, on the other hand, have given over and entrusted other things to him: almsgiving, prayers, temperance and every other virtue.[34]

On another occasion, he again speaks about the importance of Christian virtues, especially for women, who must adorn themselves "with modesty, piety, almsgiving, benevolence, love, kindliness . . . reasonableness, mildness and forbearance. These are the pigments of virtue . . . " Moreover, "the summit of virtue" is nothing else but "holiness" which leads us "to those ineffable blessings that are dispensed to those who love him."[35] These are the personal and the public virtues, the foundations of Christian virtues on interpersonal relations with God our Father and with our brothers and sisters in Christ. How much we need these virtues today . . . how much indeed! Saint John Chrysostom, the "Prophet of Charity," to use the expression of Father Florovsky, leads the way for us.[36] What Saint John Chrysostom really asked from us is that faith, charity, belief, and practice be organically linked together in the Christian way of life. We cannot claim or reject either of them.

Today we celebrate Three Hierarchs Day, which is dedicated to Greek letters and Greek paideia. Our Fathers, in the eleventh century, thought it appropriate to honor these three great hierarchs, for they combined excellent Greek education and fervent Christian commitment. Saint Basil the Great, Saint Gregory the Theologian and Saint John Chrysostom were a product of Hellenic culture, and they felt no fear in proclaiming it publically. When Julian the Apostate, with a special edict, forbade Christians to teach and to be taught Greek paideia, Saint Gregory the Theologian protested most vehemently.[37] All the Fathers, however, including Saint John Chrysostom, knew the deficiencies of pagan philosophy, and they stated it openly and publicly, but they did not reject their roots. In their writings they preserved whatever the Greek mind had produced that was beautiful and good. This is why Johannes Quasten speaks about Christianization of Hellenism.[38]

But what is more important is that above and beyond their family and their educational and spiritual background, they remained steadfast to the biblical message of Christ: love of God, and love of mankind. Christ penetrated them throughout their souls, minds, and bodies. They were truly Christocentric.

Let us conclude with a letter of Saint John Chrysostom which he wrote during one of his exiles to his friend and fellow bishop Kyriakos:

> When I was driven from the city, I felt no anxiety, but said to myself: If the empress wishes to banish me, let her do so; the earth is the Lord's. If she wants to have me sawn in sunder, I have Isaiah for an example. If she wants me to be drowned in the ocean, I think of Jonah. If I am to be thrown into the fire, the three men in the furnace suffered the same. If cast before wild beasts, I remember Daniel in the lion's den. If she wants me to be stoned, I have before me Stephen, the first martyr. If she demands my head, let her do so; John the Baptist shines before me. Naked I came from my mother's womb, naked shall I leave this world. Paul reminds me, "If I still pleased men, I would not be the servant of Christ."[39]

May the prayers and the blessing of Saint John Chrysostom and all the Three Hierarchs be with us all always. Amen.

NOTES

*An adaptation of the homily given at Vespers for the celebration of the Feast of the Three Hierarchs and Greek Letters Day at Holy Cross Chapel.

[1] See *The Writings of the Nicene and Post-Nicene Fathers*, First Series (Grand Rapids, 1956) 9, p. 22

[2] Ibid. p. 16.

[3] *The New York Times*, Sunday, January 5, 1986, p. E-19.

[4] Ibid.

[5] Ibid.

[6] Ibid.

[7] "Against Those Who Oppose the Monastic Life," 2.10, Ἕλληνες Πατέρες τῆς Ἐκκλησίας (Thessalonike, 1978) 28, p. 432.

[8] "Against Those Who Oppose the Monastic Life," ibid. 30.20, p. 589.

[9] *"On Comparison of the Royal Power and the Life of the Monk,"* ibid. 30.3, p. 597.

[10] Ibid. 30.3 and 4, p. 597ff.

[11] Ibid. 30.4, p. 607.

[12]*Homilies on Saint John,* Fathers of the Church, vol. 41 (Washington, D.C., 1960), pp. 359-60.

[13]Ibid. p. 359.

[14]Ibid. p. 360.

[15]*Homilies on Saint John,* The Fathers of the Church, Vol. 33 (Washington, D.C., 1956), p. 219.

[16]Ibid. p. 220.

[17]Ibid.

[18]Ibid. p. 221.

[19]*Homily on Saint John,* The Fathers of the Church, Vol. 39 (Washington, D.C., 1958), ibid. pp. 383-84.

[20]*On Eutropius, Patrician and Consul, Homily* 2.5. The Writings of the Nicene and Post-Nicene Fathers of the Church, vol. 9 (Grand Rapids, 1956), p. 255.

[21]*An Exhortation to Theodore after His Fall,* Letter 2, ibid. p. 114.

[22]*Second Sermon on Lazaros and the Rich Man, On Wealth and Poverty,* trans. Catherine P. Roth (Crestwood, NY, 1984), p. 49. See also Charles Avila, *Ownership: Early Christian Teaching* (Maryknoll, NY, 1983), p. 83ff.

[23]*On Virginity,* trans. Sally Rieger Shore, *Studies in Women and Religion* (New York and Toronto, 1983), p. 105. Cf. also Charles Avila, *Ownership,* pp. 85-86.

[24]*On Eutropius,* p. 254.

[25]*First Sermon on Lazaros and the Rich Man, On Wealth and Poverty,* pp. 36-37.

[26]Methodios G. F. Fouyas, *The Social Message of St. John Chrysostom* (Athens, 1968), p. 141.

[27]*On Eutropius,* p. 249.

[28]Ibid. p. 253.

[29]Ibid. p. 256.

[30]*First Sermon on Lazarus and the Rich Man, On Wealth and Poverty,* p. 37.

[31]*Saint Chrysostom, Apologist,* trans. Margaret A. Schatkin and Paul W. Harkins (Washington, D.C., 1983), p. 42.

[32]*Concerning the Statues,* Homily 4, *The Nicene and Post-Nicene Fathers,* First Series, 9, p. 365.

[33]"Baptismal Instructions", in *Ancient Christian Writers,* trans. Paul W. Harkins (Westminster, MD), p. 317. For the original text, cf. also St. John Chrysostom, Homily on Psalm 44: Ἕλληνες Πατέρες τῆς Ἐκκλησίας (Thessalonike, 1982) 6, p. 68.

[34]*Baptismal Instructions,* p. 174.

[35]Ibid. pp. 117-18.

[36]Georges Florovsky, "St. John Chrysostom: The Prophet of Charity," in *St. Vladimir's Theological Quarterly* 3 (1955) 37-42.

[37]Ibid.

[38]Ibid.

[39]*The Nicene and Post-Nicene Fathers,* First Series, 9, p. 14.

The Ecclesiastical Hierarchy of Dionysios the Areopagite: a Liturgical Interpretation

Contemporary Orthodox scholars have drawn our attention to the great value of the mystical and liturgical theology of the East.[1] The depth of Orthodox theology cannot be comprehended unless the importance and perennial relevance of this mystical and liturgical theology is grasped.

We offer this short study of the thought of Dionysios the Areopagite as a recognition not only of the author of the *Corpus Areopagiticum* but also of the perennial message of the Orthodox mystical tradition which is indeed the heart of all Orthodox theology. We believe that the *Ecclesiastical Hierarchy* of Dionysios the Areopagite is most interesting today when liturgical reforms have become imperative and when today's youth turn towards pseudo-mystical liturgical experiences in order to gratify their spiritual craving.

Although one of the most neglected works of the *Corpus Areopagiticum*, the *Ecclesiastical Hierarchy* deserves close study. It presents an important picture of the liturgical life of ancient times. At the same time it introduces us into the profound mystical interpretation of symbolism. It presents us with a most interesting theology of symbolism.

The problem of the *Corpus Areopagiticum* and the identity of Dionysios are not examined here.[2] That the *Corpus Areopagiticum* is not the work of Dionysios the Areopagite who was converted to Christianity by Saint Paul (Acts 17. 34) is not disputed any more. The author still remains a mystery. No attempt to identify the author with various prominent personalities of the early Christian era has produced successful results. There is general agreement today that the most probable date of the Pseudo-Dionysian work is between the end of the fifth century and the beginning of the sixth. The *Ecclesiastical Hierarchy* then expresses the liturgical spirit and practice of the fifth and sixth centuries.[3] As far as the geographical origin of this work is concerned, we may assume that it belongs to the Syrian rite, although it is quite difficult to prove the authenticity of this claim.[4]

This study will concentrate on the liturgy or synaxis as it is presented in the *Ecclesiastical Hierarchy*, since all the other sacraments and ecclesiastical ceremonies are centered around the eucharist as the core of the liturgical life of the Church. It is indeed interesting to note that the author of the *Ecclesiastical Hierarchy* calls the liturgy *mysterion synaxeos eitoun koinonias*. The terms *synaxis* and *koinonia* are significant because they give us immediately the proper liturgical perspective through which the author writes his Liturgy. The term synaxis means the gathering of the people of God to a certain place or *epi to auto* to use the language of Saint Ignatios of Antioch.[5] Pachymeris, the Byzantine scholar and historian of the thirtheenth century, in commenting upon the term synaxis, asserts that the word refers not so much to the gathering of the faithful in a common place but rather to the union of the people with God.[6] Pachymeris' interpretation is perhaps overly abstracted. Synaxis can include both the gathering of the faithful in order to be united among themselves in the common table of the eucharist and further the union of the faithful with God himself.[7] The use of the term koinonia strengthens this concept. Through *koinonia* or holy communion man is united both with God and with his fellow men.

The synaxis has a specific order. It starts with a "reverent prayer." Pachymeris assures that this prayer is *to eulogeton*. But we cannot be sure. The "Eulogemene he Vasileia tou Patros" (Blessed is the Kingdom of the Father) with which most of the later liturgies begin is mentioned explicity for the first time by Saint Theodore the Studite.[8]

Who is the celebrant? "The hierarch" according to Dionysios the Areopagite. And who is the hierarch? The bishop who has spiritual authority to preside in the liturgy and to direct the people of God towards the divine mysteries of the eucharist. After this "reverent prayer" the hierarch censes the whole Church. Actually we have here for the first time mention of censing as a preliminary act to the liturgy and it seems certain that before 600 A. D. censing as a liturgical act had prevailed in the East.[9]

The bishop, after the censing, returns to the altar and "begins the sacred chanting of the Psalms with the whole 'ecclesiastical order' chanting with him the sacred language of the Psalter."[10] It is obvious from this description that the *enarxis* or the beginning of the liturgy consisted of readings and chantings of the Psalms. But what does the author mean when he uses the expression "ecclesiastical order?" There is the possibility of interpreting this from our perspective to mean the clergy or even the semi-clerical orders which abounded in the early Church. But the inclusion of the laity is imperative in view of the fact that both clergy and laity were integral parts of the people of God in the early Church.[12]

After the chanting of the Psalms the reading of the lessons takes place. Maximos the Confessor interprets the phrase, *he ton hagiographon deltion anagnosis,* as the reading from the Old and New Testaments.[13] Following the readings of the lessons, the catechumens, the *energoumenoi*[14] and the penitents leave the Church. Some of the *leitourgoi*[15] stand close to the gates of the sanctuary which are now closed.[16] Immediately the deacons and priests place upon the holy altar the bread and the cup with the wine. Then all the congregation sings the *katholike hymnologia.*[17] A prayer follows by the bishop and the proclamation of peace to all. Also the kiss of love. Then the bishop reads secretly the diptychs.[18] The bishop and the priest wash their hands with water.[19] The bishop standing in the middle of the *ekkritoi*[20] proceeds with the consecration of the gifts. Here the author of the *Eccleciastical Hierarchy* does not elaborate on the procedure of the consecrating prayer but from the comments of the following chapter of Theoria one might reconstruct the main parts of the consecration.

There was a general thansgiving prayer in which the bishop would recall all the benefits which mankind had received from God up to the time of the coming of Christ whose sufferings were remembered together with the *anamnesis* of the Last Supper and the words of the institution of the holy eucharist. The elevation of the bread as well as the fraction probably took place immediately after the ceremony of the consecration. The gifts were uncovered before the consecration and were covered after it, remaining coverd until the communion.[21] The communion of the consecrated gifts followed in which all the clergy participated while the bishop exhorted the laity to participate in the sacrament. A thanksgiving prayer seems to conclude the Pseudo-Dionysian synaxis.

A comparative outline of the *synaxis* of the *Ecclesiastical Hierarchy* with its most similar liturgies, namely that of the Apostolic Constitutions[22] and of the Mystical Catechesis of Saint Cyril of Jerusalem, [23] seems useful at this point.

Dionysios the Areopagite, *Ecclesiastical Hierarchy* c. 500 A. D.	St. Cyril of Jerusalem, *Mystical Catecheses* c. 386	Apostolic *Constitutions, Book 8* c. 350-400.

SYNAXIS

1. Prayer at the altar		Reading of the O. T. and the N. T. lessons.
2. Incense of the		Sermons

whole church building		Liturgy of the Catechumens.
and the people.		Liturgy of the Faithful Prayers.
3. Chanting of Psalms		Kiss of peace
4. Reading of the O.T. and N.T. lessons		Anaphora
5. Departure of the catechumens, energoumenoi and the penitents.		Sanctus
		Anamnesis
6. Offering or proskomede of the elements on the altar.		Words of Institution
		Epiklesis
7. *Katholike Hymnologia*		Diptycha
8. Prayer, Peace to all, kiss of love.		Petitions of the deacon
		Sancta Sanctis
		Communion
9. Diptychs		Thanksgiving
10. Washing of the hands	Washing of the hands	
11. Consecration and fraction of the bread.	Kiss of peace	
	Thanksgiving	
	Sanctus	
12. Communion by the clergy and the people.	Consecration (Epiklesis)	
13. Thanksgiving.	Diptychs for the living and the dead.	
	Our Father . . .	
	Elevation of the elements or Sancta Sanctis Communion	

A study of these texts shows the Pseudo-Dionysian synaxis as simpler in form than the earlier texts of Saint Cyril and of the *Apostolic Constitutions*. Does this mean that the Dionysian text is an earlier one? There is no doubt that the liturgy of the *Ecclesiastical Hierarchy* presents an underdeveloped form of the eucharistic ceremony.

We must, however, emphasize the simplicity of this synaxis. The real value, as we shall see later, of the eucharistic sacrament lies in the mystical depth and the symbolic perspective of the whole rite. The study of its historical and practical content and of its application is useful today. At issue is not the simplistic question of whether on not we should return to a less evolved form of the eucharistic sacrament. Facing the realities of our contemporary society, the Church could make accommodations for special groups such as workers or young people. Special *synaxis* are possible. The Pseudo-Dionysian text and similar ones can serve as guides and prototypes. The "Great and Holy Synod of the Orthodox Church" has the right to study this important matter and to make decisions in the near future.

The *Ecclesiastical Hierarchy* of the Pseudo-Dionysian *Corpus* may be considered as the attempt of an early author to interpret and explain the liturgical life of the Church in a mystical manner. Is this a sign that the faithful of the author's era were already out of touch with the historical and practical meaning and purposes of the liturgical life of the Church? The *Ecclesiastical Hierarchy* is precisely the attempt to bring the early Christian faithful to a higher awareness of the meaning of the Church, to a more profound and rewarding participation in the divine life through worship.

We begin therefore our study of the material of this work by bringing into focus the mystical interpretation of the liturgy and its theological basis.

First of all, Christ himself is "the supreme divine power of every hierarchy and sanctification and divine operation."[24] Thus our author opens up the way for the exposition of his mystical theology by establishing from the very beginning that everything in fact comes from Jesus Christ. Actually Christ himself bequeathes the power of the divine priesthood from which, by approaching the holy exercise of the priestly office, we become nearer to the Being above us by assimilation, according to our power, to the stability and unchangeableness of our steadfastness in holy things. Hence by looking upwards to the blessed and supremely divine glory of Jesus and reverently gazing upon whatever we are permitted to see and being illuminated with the knowledge of the visions, we shall be able to become, as regards the science of divine mysteries, both purified and purifying-images of light, workers with God, perfect and perfecting.[25]

The christological basis of the priesthood and the absolute need of this priesthood (called "divine" by the author) for our personal illumination, purification, and finally assimilation to and union with God, are obvious here. But there is another point of great significance — the connection between the *Ecclesiastical Hierarchy* and the *Celestial Hierarchy*.

Both derive from the supreme source of all life. *Ecclesiastical Hierarchy* in particular "has one and the same power throughout the whole of its hierarchical functions, and (that) the hierarch himself according to his nature and aptitude and rank is initiated in divine things and deifies and imparts to his subordinates according to he meekness the sacred deification which comes to himself from God."[26]

The divine character of the priesthood and its divine origin is emphatically stressed. The term initiation for all the priestly functionaries is significant. It is the attempt to denote a completely new orientation for the future priest.

The *celestial hierarchy* of course is "intellectual" and "supermundane" (*note kai hyperkosmios hestin*). In contrast, the *Ecclesiastical Hierarchy* "conformable to our nature, abounds in a manifold variety of material symbols from which, in proportion to our capacity, we are conducted by sacerdotal function to the one-like deification, assimilation to God and the divine virtue."[27] So the author is a practical man and he wants to make clear his point that the ecclesiastical hierarchy, the priesthood on earth needs "material symbols" in order to exercise its duties. Symbolism therefore has a practical purpose and it accords with our human nature.

But one question naturally arises. Namely what is the ecclesiastical hierarchy of which the author so aptly speaks? "Our hierarchy is the systematic account of the whole sacred rites included in it (and) according to which the divine hierarch, being initiated, will have within himself the participation of the most sacred things as chief of (the) hierarchy."[28]

And even more precisely the author assures us that "as he who speaks of (the) hierarchy speaks of (the) order of the whole sacred rites collectively so he who mentions (the) hierarch denotes an inspired and godly man, one who understands accurately all sacred knowledge, in whom is completed and recognized in his purity the whole hierarchy."[29]

Thus, the earthly basis of the role of the hierarchy is maintained, the collective mission of the clergy is established, the whole range of the Christian sacrament is embraced and the deifying purpose of the whole hierarchy is again expounded. This last point is made clear when the author again writes: "Deification is the assimilation and oneness towards God as far as permissible. Now this is the common love of every hierarchy — the clinging love towards God and divine things: a love divinely sanctified into oneness with him."[30]

But then what is the main difference between the celestial and the ecclesiastical hierarchies? It is apparent that God has used for the celestial hierarchy immaterial and intellectual means whereas for our own ecclesiastical hierarchy God has provided the *theoparadota logia,* the God-given words, "in a variety and multitude of divisible symbols as we are able to receive them."[31]

In fact these "God-given words" were given from our inspired in-itiators, *entheon hieroteleston,* in divinely written letters of the Word of God. It seems that Dionysios refers here to the Old and the New Testaments. For Dionysios the very essence of our hierarchy is these "God-given words."[32] Besides these written words there is also oral tradition which was transmitted from mind to mind through the medium of speech.[33] But we must remember that our hierarchs transmit these things not in clear and understandable means but in sacred symbols.[34] The whole concept of *disciplina arcani* or the discipline of secrecy comes to mind[35] and more especially Saint Basil's unwritten, unpublished or secret tradition.[36]

Then the author of the *Corpus Areopagiticum* proceeds to the special orders or the sacred orders which are within the ecclesiastical hierarchy. These orders are in fact threefold and are arranged "as first, middle, and last in rank, each carefully guarding the proportion of religious rites, and the well-ordered fellowship which keeps in harmonious order and binds all things together."[37]

The sacerdotal order is also divided in the following way into three parts: "into a purifying, and illuminating, and perfecting discipline."[38] The first of the sacred or contemplative orders is the divine order of the hierarchs or bishops. The hierarchs are those who work for the perfec-tion of all things in the ecclesiastical hierarchy. As Jesus Christ is the model of both the ecclesiastical and the celestial hierarhies so all the orders have their ultimate authority in the office of the hierarch. He is "the power of the hierarchical order (which) permeates the whole sacred body and through every one of the sacred orders performs the mysteries of its proper hierarchy."[39]

The hierarch has the right and the privilege to perform most of the services in the sanctuary. In fact, the priest can do nothing unless he is designated, *kekleromenos,* by the hierarch. The latter can perform or-dination, the consecration of the divine *myron,* and the complete con-secration of the altar. The "perfecting faculty" is given to the hierarchs.[40]

The order of priests is the "illluminating order" (*photagokike taxis*).[41]

They conduct and advise the initiated and co-operate with the hierarch in the sacraments. The "leitourgoi" or the deacons are the "purifying order." They separate the unit before the liturgy and "purify those (who) are drawing nigh, making them entirely pure from opposing fashions, and suitable for the sanctifying vision and communion.''[42]

The deacons help those who are to become Christians to renounce their former life, and they teach them the new way of life. This function is expressed symbolically at the sacrament of baptism by the assistance they give in removing the candidate's clothing.

The author reminds us that the practical functions of the sacred orders are in reality images of the divine energies and therefore are arranged ''in hierarchical distinctions showing in themselves the regulated illuminations into the first, middle, and last sacred divine energies.''[43]

The intent of the analogy becomes most clear when the author states that the hierarchical image follows in its threefold division the Supreme Diety himself who first cleanses the minds which he enters, then enlightens, and when enlightened brings them to a Godlike perfection.[44]

The ceremonies of ordination of the three ranks of the hierarchy are described by the author in only a few words. The same procedure is followed for the three ranks: the procession to the altar, kneeling, the imposition of the hierarch's right hand, the cruciform seal, the announcement of the name, and the completion of the salutation.[45]

Behind all these acts there is a mystical meaning. The procession, for instance, to the altar together with the kneeling, suggests that the ordained person places his life, his ''whole intellectual self'' under God, who is the real author of the consecration, and approaches him pure and hallowed. The imposition of the hierarch's right hand signifies the protection of the primal consecrator by whom, as holy children, they are cherished paternally. It gives them at the same time, (the sacerdotal habit and function) and drives away the opposing power.[46] The sign of the cross has its own symbolic meaning; it signifies and manifests the inaction of the impulses of the flesh. The calling aloud of the name of the ordained signifies that his choice was made by God himself and not by the hierarch. The salutation (kiss) points to the mutual love among those who are in the same rank and also the religious communion of minds of like character.[47] Finally the author presents a mystical interpretation for each distinctive mark of the ordination of each rank. On the future hierarch's head the Gospels are placed, signifying that through his office, he leads those who have been purified by the deacons and enlightened by the priests to the knowledge which makes perfect the new Christians.[48]

So much for the sacred order of the ecclesiastical hierarchy. What of the mystical and symbolic meaning of the sacraments of baptism and of chrism? Here the author has many things to say. First for the author:

"the earliest approach towards the religious performance of the divine commandments is the unutterable creation of our being in God."[49] We must be taught the way we are going to obtain our "regeneration." Actually the center of illumination is the union with Christ "like as by fire to assimilate things that have been made one, in proportion to their aptitude of deification."[50]

Union with Christ therefore and deification are the ultimate goals of baptism. The rite of baptism follows the well-known traditional line: Thanksgiving by the hierarch, hymn sung by the whole body of the Church, confession by the future Christian, imposition of the hierarch's hand upon his head, and his registration and that of his sponsor by the priests. After a prayer the deacons remove from the baptized his old clothes and sandals. He turns to the west and renounces Satan three times and once again recites his confession three times. The priest anoints his entire body with the oil while the bishop dedicates the water by sacred invocation and consecrates it by three cruciform affusions of holy myron. Baptism then follows whereupon the bishop immerses the baptized into the water three times invoking the name of the Holy Trinity. Then he is clothed and is anointed with chrism by the bishop after which he receives, for the first time, holy communion.[51]

There is much beauty and profound meaning behind the simple but very impressive acts. The author writes: "This initiation of the holy birth in God, as in symbols, has nothing unbecoming or irreverent, not anything of sensible imagery, but enigmas of a contemplation worthy of God, bearing a likeness to natural images suitable to men."[52]

At this point Dionysios feels that it would be relevent to clear up any misunderstanding which could arise from the manner and method of his interpretation. He writes: "Sensible sacred things are reliefs of things intelligible to which they lead and show the way. But things intellegible are archetype and explanation of sacred things cognizable by the senses."[53]

Thus having explained his method: the philosophical and theological basis upon which he builds his interpretation, the author proceeds to the mystical meaning of baptism. The bishop's seal upon the initiated in a sign or a symbol of the divine blessedness which imparts to him divine light and makes him a godly sharer of the inheritance and of the sacred order of godly men. The neophyte's registration (as well as that of his sponsor) by the priests is a sign that he belongs to those who are in the process of salvation. The holy anointing and the holy oil prepare the neophyte in his struggle against death and destruction and build him up into a victorious athlete who can support his freedom and his spiritual strength against death and destruction.[54] The three immersions in the water symbolize the three days and nights which Christ spent in the tomb.[55] The white garments are the light which his image should always reflect.[56] The most perfecting unction or the myrrh makes the neophyte a person of "good odor" of good fragrance.[57] It gives to him also the indwelling of the supremely divine Spirit.[58]

We come now to the part of the *Ecclesiastical Hierarchy* which is most important for this present study: the synaxis and holy communion.

Earlier we discussed the form and the order of the synaxis.[59] Let us look now at the mystical interpratation our author gives us. First of all the general and peaceful distribution of one and same bread and of one and the same cup signifies a fellowship in spirit, and the provision of spiritual nourishment for the faithful. It is a memorial of the Mystical Supper of our Lord. Thus, the synaxis has a unique, simple, and pro-scribed origin. Liturgically, it is multiplied into a holy variety of symbols and allows us to travel through the whole range of divine imagery.[60] Our author deals specifically with these.

The singing of the Psalms for instance signifies the harmonious condition of our souls during the celebration of the mystery. Contemplating on the scripture readings, the congregated are inspired as "being moved by the one supremely divine Spirit."[61] The reading of the diptychs and the kiss of peace symbolize the unity of all the faithful "for it is not possible to be collected to the One and to partake of the peaceful Oneness of the One when people are divided among themselves."[62] The reading of diptychs also signifies the inseparable conjuction of the celestial and the ecclesiastical orders in Christ our Lord.[63] With the washing of the hands the hierarch is made like Christ clean and spotless[64] and con-secrates and distributes the "divine symbols" as Christ did himself at the Last Supper.[65] The breaking of the Bread and the distribution of the Cup are acts according to which "he symbolically multiplies and distributes the unity completing in these a most holy divine service."[66] By bringing the veiled gifts to view, the bishop brings forth Christ from the "hiddenness of the Father."[67] With the distribution of the gifts to all the faithful, Christ calls them into communion with himself and his own good things.

Dionysios' mystical interpretation of the eucharist is a magnificent one. His symbolism directs our attention to a higher reality. It is a focus about which the whole life of the faithful must move and develop.

Our author goes to the deep mystical meaning of the whole Christian life. He deals with the life of the monks. The sacred order of monks is made up of men who must live a life of purification. Monks in fact have acquired a spiritual ascent to contemplation and the participation in every divine service.[68] There is a special ceremony for the consecration of the monk which is very simple. The candidate kneels and the hierarch imposes his hand. The priest blesses him and makes the sign of the cross upon him and crops his hair.

Some conclusions should be drawn at the end of this study. First, the *Ecclesiastical Hierarchy* is one of the most important liturgical texts of the early Christian period, and it introduces us, in a rather simple way, to the liturgical life and praxis of the Church of the fifth and sixth centuries. It expresses the liturgical ethos of the Syrian rite. It includes primitive elements from the life of the early Church, yet it shows us the tendency of that time for further elaboration of the liturgical life. However, the author's primary concern is not so much with an exact description of the liturgical ceremonies of his time or of this land. His purpose is not to offer a complete and detailed liturgical text. Rather it is to present to his reader a commentary on, and an interpretation of the liturgical life of his time. His approach is philosophical, theological, and mystical Dionysios is a profound thinker, a possessor of an excellent philosophical education. His sharp mind and his mystical intuition are inter-mingled to provide for a grasp of the more inward plane of the spiritual life. He succeeds in transforming texts, words, and ceremonies into an abiding source of inspiration for all the faithful. Young people of today would find in him an endless source of pure Christian mysticism and the flames of his spirituality can touch and move many cynical hearts of our time. He links the celestial and the ecclesiastical hierarchies admirably into the supreme an absolute oneness of Christ and establishes a common source and a common goal of both heavenly and earthly beings. He walks on the earth, so to speak, but he flies in heaven with an astonishing assurance, with wholesome faith and sincere love. His analogies and parallelisms are instructive even to our practical minds. Thus the role of the ecclesiastical hierarchy, though symbolically stated is clearly defined: "For thus our hierarchy, reverently arranged in ranks fixed by God, is the heavenly hierarchy, preserving, so far as man can do, its Godlike characteristics and divine imitation."[75]

Parker claims that he has traced Platonic influence in the language and the context of the Dionysian text. Now the Platonic influence on Dionysios has become a subject of disputes and controversies. There is no doubt that he used Neo-Platonic sources, as Father Florovsky has already stated,[76] and sometimes this extensive use of Neo-Platonic sources and language is an impediment in making his thought clear. But thers is no doubt that he remains a Christian theologian as both Father

Florovsky[77] and Vladimir Lossky[78] have proved. One must also remember that he succeeds in transforming Neo-Platonic terminology into Christian vocabulary. The use of words like *teleosis, catharsis, theourgia, noete, theorea, meesis, archetypon, enosis methexis*, were in use as philosophical terms of his times and there is no doubt that Dionysios, whoever he may be, succeeded in Christianizing this Greek termionology.

In studying the *Ecclesiastical Hierarchy* in particular and the whole *Corpus Areopagiticum* in general, one can see that Dionysios' main concern is the union of man with God. This union is a complete union, a perfect participation in the divine energies of god and this is the basic substratum as well as the ultimate goal of Dionysios' mystical theology. How can we reach this perfet union? Through the *Ecclesiastical Hierarchy*, the author answers: Here precisely lies the center around which the Christian sacraments move. Nonetheles, he is conscious of the dangers which might spring out of this thesis. Therefore. he is ready to proclaim that "if we aspire to communion with him, we must keep our eyes fixed upon his most godly life in the flesh, and we must retrace our path to the Godlike and blameless habit of mind by being made like it in holy sinlessness. For thus he will communicate to us an harmonious likeness to himself."[79]

Dionysios seems to be a Christ-centered man and a man who knows the necessity of combining divine grace and human efforts in the attainment of deification. But above all Dionysios' contribution to Christian thought is found mainly in his mystical approach and intuition which are expressed in the whole spectrum of his theology and in introducing the mystical interpretation into the sphere of the liturgical life of the Church.

Dionysios, the unknown author, remains one of the outstanding theologians of the early Church. Through, the breath of a sincere and profound mystical theology, he offers us an insight into the hierarchical structure of all human life and of the whole cosmos; that, in fact, is the common denominator in all stratas of life is divine. His *Ecclesiastical Hierarchy* proves his awareness of the need for order in all expressions of life. The liturgical praxis of the Church is a necessary part of his work.

But for contemporary man his message is more sound and clear: He shows us that only through a pure and simple liturgical experience can we attain our ultimate goal — perfection.

NOTES

[1]See Georges Florovsky's very interesting and informative article on Dionysios the Areopagite in the *Threskeutike kai Ethike Egkyklopaideia* (Athens, 1968), p. 47-80.

[2]For a complete bibliography on Dionysios see ibid., p. 480; *Real-lexikon für Antike und Christentum*, pp. 1075-1121; and B. Altaner, *Patrology* (Edinburgh and London, 1960), pp. 604-09.

[3]G. Florovsky, *Egkyklopaideia*; J. Tixeront, *A Handbook of Patrology* (St. Louis and London, 1943), p. 289; and J. Quasten, *Monumenta eucharistica et liturgica vetustissima* (Bonn, 1938), p. 275.

[4]Ibid., p. 275 and G. Dix, *The Shape of the Liturgy* (Glasgow, 1954), p. 445.

[5]*Letter to the Ephesians*, ch. 5.

[6]PG 3.452.

[7]At least this appears to be the conclusion of Dionysios' introduction to the Synaxis and Pachymeris himself; PG.3. 421 an 452.

[8]In this "Hermenia tes Leitourgias ton Progiasmenon," PG 99.1690.

[9]Dix, *Liturgy*, pp. 444-46.

[10]*Ecclesiastical Hierarchy*, 3.2. We use the translation of J. Parker, *The Celestial and Ecclesiastical Hierarchy of Dionysios the Areopagite* (London, 1894).

[11]The Greek expression is *ekklesiastike diakosmesis* which more precisely means "ecclesiastical ornamentation" or "decoration."

[12]Sait Ignatios, *Letter to the Ephesians*, ch. 5, 9, 13. Cf. also *Letter to Magnesians*, ch. 4, 6, 7.

[13]PG 4. 136B.

[14]*Energoumenoi*, i.e. those who are annoyed by demons. Cf. also *Apostolic Constitutions, 8*, 7, 9 and Maximos the Confessor, PG 4.136B.

[15]The term *leitourgoi* is explained by Maximos the Confessor as being the deacons and the sub-deacons. Ibid, Pachymeris refers only to the sub-deacons; PG 3.452D.

[16]*Para tas tou hierou pelas sigkekleismenas.* It seems that the word *hierou* means sanctuary, at least if one looks at the text superficially. But gates were not in existence at that time, since the *iconostasion* in the present form had not been developed yet. We are inclined to believe that the author refers to the gates of the whole church building.

[17]It has been assumed that this *katholike hymnologia* was actuallly the Creed. Maximos the Confessor PG 3. 352 and Pachymeris PG 4.136 accept this interpretation. Later, however, it was assumed that it was a hymn or the ektenis recited by the deacon or even the Doxology. Metropolitan Athenagoras thinks that *Katholike hymnologia* is in reality nothing less but a form of Doxology as it is found in the Liturgy of the Apostolic Constitutions. See Metropolitan Athenagoras, "Hen leitourgikon provlema," *Ekklesiastikos Pharos* 32 (1933), pp. 9-51.

[18]As we see here the diptychs were read before the consecration, a custom which was not prevalent in the East before the 4th century. Cf. G. Dix, *Liturgy*, p. 498, and P. Trembelas, *Hoi, Treis Leitourgiai* (Athens, 1935), p. 117.

[19]Cf. for comments and interpretation of Dionysios in *Theoria*, ch. 3. It symbolizes the cleansing which should be the characteristic act of the clergy's whole life.

[20]Maximos explains that these are deacons. He also refers to the custom in Rome according to which seven deacons only should participate in the liturgy. PG 4.136. Here we have the Offering or Proskomede and the Great Entrance. All are combined in one act.

[21]Cf. Maximos the Confessor, *Scholia*, PG 4.137A.

[22]The text in Quasten, *Monumenta eucharistica.*

[23]The text edited by Frank Cross, *St. Cyril of Jerusalem's Lectures on the Christian Sacraments* (London, 1951), p. 26ff.

[24]*Ecclesiastical Hierarchy*, 1.1

[25]Ibid.

[26]Ibid.

[27]Ibid.

[28]Ibid. 1.111

[29]Ibid.

[30]Ibid.

[31]Ibid. 1.4. Parker (Hierarchy, p. 52) translates the word logia as oracles. We do not feel that this translation is accurate.

[32]*Ecclesiastical Hierarchy*, 1.4.

[33]Cf. Maximos the Confessor. PG 4.120-21.

[34]*Ecclesiastical Hierarchy* 1, 1.4.

[35]Cf. my paper: "The Concept of Tradition in the Fathers of the Church" in *The Greek Orthodox Theological Review*, 15 (1970).

[36]*On the Holy Spirit*, ch. 27.

[37]*Ecclesiastical Hierarchy*, 5, ch. 2.

[38]Ibid. 5.3.

[39]Ibid. 5.5.

[40]Ibid. 5.6.

[41]Ibid.

[42]Ibid.

[43]Ibid. 5.7.

[44]Ibid.

[45]Ibid. 5.2.3.

[46]Ibid.

[47]Ibid. 5.4.5.

[48]Ibid. 5.7.8.

[49]Ibid. 2 (Introduction).

[50]Ibid. 2.1.

[51]Ibid. 2.5.6.7.

[52]Ibid. 2.1.3.

[53]Ibid. 2.3.2.

[54]Ibid. 2.3.6.

[55]Ibid. 2.3.7.

[56]Ibid. 2.3.8.
[57]Ibid.
[58]Ibid. 4.3.11.
[59]Cf. pp. 2-5.
[60]Ecclesiastical Hierarchy, ch. 3.3.3.
[61]Ibid. 3.3.4.
[62]Ibid. 3.3.8.
[63]Ibid. 3.3.9.
[64]Ibid. 3.3.10.
[65]Ibid. 3.3.12.
[66]Ibid.
[67]Ibid. 3.3.13.
[68]Ibid. 6.1.3.
[69]Ibid.
[70]Ibid. 6.3.4.
[71]Ibid. 8.1.1.
[72]Ibid. 7.7.
[73]Ibid. 8.3.8.
[74]Ibid. 7.3.9.
[75]Ibid.
[76]Florovsky, *Egkyklopaideia*, col. 479.
[77]Ibid., col. 476.
[78]Vladimir Lossky, *The Mystical Theology of the Eastern Church* (London, 1957), pp. 37ff, 139ff.
[79]*Ecclesiastical Hierarchy, 3.3.12.*

Saint Photios as
an Orthodox Theologian and Scholar

Apolytikion

Being like-minded to the Apostles and a teacher of the whole world, O Photios, intercede with the Master of all that he may grant peace to the world and great mercy to our souls.

O man of God, faithful servant, minister of the Lord, minister of inspiration, chosen vessel, pillar and foundation of the Church, heir of the kingdom, peer of the Apostles, confessor and defender of Orthodox doctrine, refuter of soul-destroying heresy, O great Photios, cease not to cry out to the Lord for us.

With these beautiful words, the hymnographer of the Church expresses the feelings of the people of God towards Saint Photios, a holy Ecumenical Patriarch of Constantinople during the ninth century. Saint Photios the Great is considered to be a pillar of the Church, a defender of the Orthodox faith, and a peer of the Apostles. He embodies the spirit of the Scriptures, the theology of the Fathers who preceded him, as well as the true liturgical experience of the Church. He is thus an example of the Orthodox theologian par excellence. In his famous encyclical to the patriarchs of the East, he epitomizes in one striking sentençe the essence of his theology: "Do not abandon the order established by the holy Fathers which they, by their acts and deeds, handed down to us as a legacy to preserve."[1] Writing to Pope Nicholas I, Saint Photios clearly states the theological basis upon which his life and thought are built: "Nothing is dearer than the truth," and, "It is truly necessary that we observe all things, but, above all, that which pertains to matters of the faith, in which but a small deviation represents a deadly sin."[2] Indeed, Saint Photios has been and still is one of the greatest personalities of the Byzantine era. The impact of his work has not only left its marks on the ninth century, but on the whole course of secular and ecclesiastical history. We would be within the limits of scholarly accuracy if we said that our church now lives in the post-Photian era; for his times are in reality the starting point of a new period within the history of the Church which is comprised of a victorious consolidation and a new epoch of self-retrospection and self-evaluation.

Saint Photios was a son of a noble Byzantine family of ancient Armenian stock which was related to the Macedonian royal dynasty. Because of his noble status, he had the opportunity to enter into the high ranks of the imperial court and to serve as a top-ranking diplomat and ambassador to Assyria for Emperor Michael III (842-867). Next, he was appointed as the first imperial secretary of the royal court, and thus Saint Photios soon acquired power and glory in the imperial palace of Constantinople. He also became the prime minister of Emperor Michael III, and at the same time he reorganized and taught at the celebrated University of Constantinople, two tasks which could not have been easy even for a man of the stature of the holy Photios. Yet he became famous, as well as one of the most imposing and controversial personalities of his times when he was elected and consecrated archbishop and patriarch of Constantinople in 858.

This great man, bishop, and theologian of wondrous biblical roots, of exquisite theological acumen, of rare erudition and sincere piety became a controversial figure and faced many adversaries and enemies during his lifetime. Perhaps the most antagonistic issue was whether his election and ordination as patriarch was canonical. Many of his contemporaries wrote against him, such as Niketas of Paphlagonia, the metropolitan of Smyrna; Stylianos of Neocaesarea, Pope Nicholas I and Anastasios the Librarian, just to mention a few. They presented him as an unscrupulous and covetous man, as a person blinded by pride and a lust for power. Later, a whole stream of historians, especially in the West, depicted him as a man of ambition, pride, bias and theological scholarship. They claimed that his actions led to the rift and the schism between East and West. Baronius, the celebrated Western historian of the seventeenth century, Cardinal Hergerther of the nineteenth century, in his work *Photius Patriarch of Constantinople*, and the French historian E. Amman painted a malevolent picture of Saint Photios, ignoring the true dimensions of his character while distorting the historical evidence which was at their disposal. Yet even his most fierce enemies could not dismiss the nobility of his character, his splendid education, and his great contribution to teaching and writing. Thus, Niketas of Paphlagonia, who was not a friend of his, writes:

> Photios was not of low and obscure origins; rather, he was the child of noble and highly renowned parents. In worldly wisdom and reasoning, he was viewed as the most capable person in the Empire. He had studied grammar and poetry, rhetoric and philosophy, the healing arts [apparently medicine], and almost every other worldly science. In all of these, he not only surpassed all others of his time, but even competed with learned men of earlier times. He succeeded in all things, and all things benefited him: his natural capabilities, his diligent learning, and his wealth by which every book was able to find its way to him.[3]

Later serious and unbiased scholars, such as Laport, Grumel, and, finally, Dvornik realized that the history of Saint Photios needed to be rewritten and that all the anti-Photian documents upon which his condemnation was based demanded thorough inspection and revision. The man who fully reopened Photios' dossier and re-examined his case was Francis Dvornik in his celebrated book, *The Photian Schism, History and Legend*. He based his work on solid historical evidence and proved that Patriarch Photios has wrongly stood as a sign of contradiction, a symbol of disunion, and the father of the schism between the East and the West. Thus, no serious scholar today challenges Saint Photios' moral character and his deep devotion to the Church and her unity.

He lived during one of the most enlightened periods of Medieval Hellenism, for during the ninth century a new vigorous impetus was given to Greek paideia. During the reign of Emperor Michael III, the prime minister Bardas reopened the University of Constantinople with Saint Photios as its director. It was during this period that lowercase letters were used in manuscripts, and the clergy and the laity developed a great interest in both the classical tradition and the physical sciences (mathematics, geometry, astronomy, etc.), and, thus, the ninth century continued the cultivation of Hellenic culture in a most energetic way. During this century, though, it was primarily due to Photios that a new rediscovery of the Classics takes place, a rediscovery which actually leads to a reexamination of the relationship of the ancient Greek classical tradition to Christian life and Christian literature. In other words, in Saint

Photios, ancient Greek tradition and classical heritage are Christianized and combined with the Christian faith in order to produce a new synthesis of Hellenic-Christian paideia. Saint Photios' books contain ample and abounding examples of his absolute and complete familiarity with both classical philosophy and philology, as well as Christian tradition.

While prime minister, he wrote his well-known book *Amphilochia*, a book written at the request of his friend Amphilochios, bishop of Kyzikos, in which he answers three hundred and twenty-six questions and problems drawn from holy Scripture. Other books of his that should be mentioned are his most celebrated *On the Mystagogy of the Holy Spirit, Against the Manicheans*, and his *Nomocanon*, a collection and interpretation of church canons and laws. He wrote and compiled church hymns and songs, and also wrote commentaries on the letters of the holy apostle Paul, called *Explanation of the Letters of Saint Paul.* Indeed, Saint Photios was a proficient biblical scholar and a pious reader of Scripture. In his most celebrated book, *On the Mystagogy of the Holy Spirit*, there are fifty-three quotations from both the Old and New Testaments. There he discusses at length the *filioque* which he finds to be against "the dogmas of our common Savior and Creator and Lawgiver," against "the word of the Savior." "It strives to change the medicine of the Lord's doctrine into an unspeakably dead poison." "The Son himself delivers his mystical teaching that the Spirit proceeds from the Father."[4] The "filioque" is against "the Master's ordinances," against "the Master's mystagogy."[5] Writing to Pope Nicholas I, Saint Photios writes again that no one can dare to despise and scorn "the dogmas of the Lord, the Fathers, and the Councils."[6] Repeatedly, Saint Photios speaks about the Scriptures, the Fathers, the canons, and the councils of the Church as the correct criteria of the Orthodox faith.

Here his whole attitude towards Orthodoxy enters into the picture. Patriarch Photios was Orthodox because he was profoundly historically minded. He had indeed a strong sense of the linear process of history, and he had been involved in the philosophical and theological interpretations of history. He was very much interested in history as such and in the historical method as an emperical and scientific means of interpreting Orthodox theology. He knew all the great thinkers of ancient Greece and he extensively used all the techniques of logical reasoning, as well as mathematics and dialectics to serve his theological purposes. He knew that the Christian epoch was a new epoch which was beyond the ancient Greek era. The Christian epoch included the Scriptures, the Fathers of the Church, and the ecumenical synods which are all links in the chain of historical continuity. Thus, historical tradition for Saint Photios is the "sina qua non" of the Christian Church. Out of his conviction that any departure from historical tradition leads to the violation of the unity of the Church and to the tragic loss of the ecumenical view of the Christian life came his polemics against the Romans and the Bulgarians for their doctrinal innovations and his attacks against the Arians and the Iconoclasts.

Vasiliev considers the most important contribution of Saint Photios to the history of the Church to be that "in his lifetime and as a result of his influence, a closer and more friendly relation developed between secular science and theological teaching." On the other hand, Krumbacher does not consider Saint Photios' theology to be the most beautiful leaf in the crown of his glorious personality. He does recognize, however, that he was a man from whom history is borne through the spirit of his times and his individual characteristics. Williston Walker, in his voluminous book on the history of the Christian Church which is used as an indispensible text in many Protestant seminaries, devotes only a few lines to the great and holy Photios. What does this mean for the contemporary Orthodox student? Is Saint Photios still relevant in the contemporary Christian Church?

Saint Photios was not a theologian of books, but a pious man of both secular and sacred letters and wisdom. We must not forget that we live in a period when the history of the Christian Church is dismissed altogether. The proclamation of the so-called social Gospel and "God is dead" theology are signs of the anti-historical spirit currently prevailing in contemporary Christian thought. The greatest blow against history in general and ecclesiastical history in particular has been given by the eminent French scholar and ethnologist Claude Levi Strauss. In his theory of structuralism, he maintained that there is not one history, but a multitude of histories interpreted by the many types of existing mythologies, and thus man is actually responding to programmed circuits called structures. The individual conscience is no longer relevant. The whole body of Western thought from Plato to Descartes and Sartre, which holds that knowledge of the world begins with the knowledge of oneself, belongs in the natural history museum. Thus, first of all, Saint Photios reminds us of the value and purpose of history. He points out to us that classical philosophy and Christan tradition are both parts of history, and in denying them, we deny the dynamic process of the Church in the world and her saving and redeeming power for man. No history! No salvation! Thus must be our premise and presupposition in confronting the secular thought of our times. Saint Photios gives us a fine example. He was a man of history, a man of the world, a classical scholar, a mathematician, a monk, a diplomat, a prolific writer, and a patriarch, a man of the experience of history. To use his own words, above all things, he was a man of faith. He was committed to Christ, his Church, and his flock.

He knew and espoused in his life the famous dictum "the heart makes the theologian." Above and beyond all, he was a man of love, a man of forgiveness. He wrote to Pope Nicholas I:

> Nothing is more honorable and precious than love, as both common opinion recognizes and the Holy Spirit witnesses, for by love the divided are united and the estranged reconciled. Love is that which unites and presses its own closer to itself. For love "thinks no evil," rather, it "bears all things, endures all things" and according to the blessed Saint Paul, "never fails." Love makes true friends of those who have the same faith in God, although distance separates them . . . Therefore, beloved ones, let us diligently cleave to love. Let us pursue it earnestly; let us take it in our homes; let us make it our companion in marketplaces, in places of seclusion, in cities, in the wilderness, in councils, in tribunals. . . . For it is the source of long-sufferings, of kindness, of lenience, of absence of anger, of meekness, of faith, of hope, of patience.[7]

This is why Saint Photios was ready to accept the diversity and variety of the religious and ecclesiastical customs of the Latins, Slavs, Bulgarians, and of all people who have the same faith, but live the Hellenic medieval ecclesiastical and social structure differently.

Also, holy Photios knew and practiced humility. In this same letter to Pope Nicholas I, he speaks about his forced election to the patriarchal throne. He writes:

> Nothing hinders brothers from speaking to one another, and children can speak boldly to their fathers if only they speak the truth. Therefore, I will say something in my own defense. First of all, that your Excellency should sympathize with me, I was forced against my will to take on the burden, so do not accuse me of seeking it. For truly, I experienced force, of what kind and how much only God knows, to whom even the deepest secrets are known. I was violently beseiged on all sides, and they watched me as if they were about to commit a crime; I was elected, even though I declined; I was consecrated, even though I wept. Everyone saw all of this and knows it, for it did not happen in a corner somewhere but in the open.[8]

Such is the way that this humble bishop of our Church wrote. Added to this genuine sense of humility is his absolute devotion to the doctrine of the Holy Trinity and of Christ.

He is christological and christocentric in all his writings. In his sermon from the *ambon* of the great church of Hagia Sophia, he first speaks about the doctrine of the Holy Trinity. He writes:

> But piously professing the Trinity to be consubstantial, of the same throne and of the same nature to itself, let us maintain in correct faith the identity of the Father, Son, and Holy Spirit unmingled, believing the Father to be unbegotten, the Son unbegotten, and the Holy Spirit emanated. . . . Thinking and believing in this wise, let us spit upon all heretical company, and abominate every schismatic wickedness. Let us hate mutual dissensions, remembering the foregoing, and how great a harvest of evils internal seditions begat. Let none among you say, "I am of Paul, and I of Cephas (1 Cor 1.12) and I of this man or of that." Christ has redeemed us from the curse of the law by his own blood: we are of Christ and bear the name. Christ was crucified for us, suffered death, was buried and arose, that he might unite them that stand wide and apart, having divinely established one baptism, one faith, and one catholic and apostolic Church. This is the core of Christ's coming among men. . . . [9]

So the theology of Saint Photios stands on solid Orthodox ground. His love for the Church is boundless. He speaks about "the beauty" and the "splendor" of the Church, and he defends the Orthodox clergy who labor within her. He states that priests and bishops have both suffered slanders and calumnies from impious men. Yet he also says that if a shepherd is a heretic,

> then he is a wolf, and it will be needful to flee and leap away from him, and not be deceived into approaching him, even if he appears to be fawning gently. Avoid communion and intercourse with him as snake's poison. But if the bishop or shepherd is orthodox, "then submit to him, since he presides in the likeness of Christ . . . [10]

We have eighteen preserved homilies of the holy Photios which are proof of his deep religious feelings and his unquestionable devotion which many of us today lack. To use Archibald Macleish's words, we know more than any previous generation and probably feel less, and it is our incapacity to feel, to realize emotionally what we know intellectually that

is at the root of our trouble. Slavery begins when men give up trying
to know with the whole human heart. The man who knows with his mind
only has no freedom anywhere. Sooner or later his life will seem more
indifferent to him. In these homilies, Saint Photios has expressed his
love and devotion to the Virgin Mary many times. We have the sermons
he preached on the feastdays of the Nativity of the Virgin Mary as well
as the Annunciation. Most of his sermons end with a request for the media-
tion and the intercessions of the ever-virgin Mother of God. Especially
noteworthy is his homily on the Annunciation, preached on March 25,
865, which ends with moving prayers to the Virgin Mary, the Mother
of God.

At the same time, we must not forget that Saint Photios has been
a great champion of the veneration of the holy icons. He very pertinently
asks:

> Does a man hate the teaching through pictures? Then how had he
> not previously rejected the hated message of the Gospels? Thus,
> speech, hearing, and seeing are parts of the religious edification of
> the Christians. The argument is indisputable. If you do not accept
> the images as a part of the sacred history of God, you cannot accept
> the Holy Scripture itself.[11]

Yet the theology of Saint Photios is not simply a theology of faith,
but is also a theology of praxis. Speaking about the spiritual life, he reminds
us that we possess the fountain of tears, that most excellent and most
beneficial thing, which drips down the cheeks, yet washes splendidly the
soul . . . and waters Paradise to bear fruits for us. We have the remedy
of tears as a means of repentance and as a way of cleasing our souls. Tears
offer "a sweet fragrance" and "they blot out the stains and scars" of
our souls. Moreover, tears "extinguish the unquenchable fire of that ter-
rifying and awful hell, and win the dew of Paradise."[12]

Writing to Prince Boris of Bulgaria, Saint Photios reminds him, and
us as well, that:

> sensible and stable men, whenever they are successful, do not become
> conceited, but restrain any pride in their success and assuage the anger
> of those who are envious of them. Whenever they stumble, however,
> they bear up bravely, and making that which has happened to them
> a foundation for their virtue, they strengthen their resolve and banish
> despondency from their minds; for they are aware of the uncertainty
> of human affairs. It is a sign of folly, vanity, and vulgarity to be

puffed up by one's successes, to take with ill grace one's failure, and to wallow in despondency.[13]

He also writes concerning vanity and the futility of life:

Attend, therefore, brethren and comprehend how paltry our life is, how quickly it withers, that it is compared to a shadow and allocated to dreams, and is found to be no more stable than any of those. For our life here passes by while it seems to be present, and once it has passed, does not return, but measured out and flowing away with the current of time, it combines the stationary with the passing, existence with non-existence, corruption with generation. Let us consider who we are, and no matter how long we may live here, whither we shall go hereafter, and how, unavoidably, we shall pay penalties for our deeds in this life, and let us not attach ourselves to this present life only, but let us be mindful of the life to come.[14]

Writing to the emperor Basil who sent him into exile, the holy Photios protests vehemently that they deprived him of his books. "Why have the books been taken away from us?" And he concludes this emotionally written letter to the emperor, "Remember that you are a human being, even though you are the emperor. Remember that we are clothed with the same flesh, whether we are kings or private persons, and that we share the same nature. Remember that we have a common Master and Fashioner and a common Judge.[15]

As Saint Photios was a practical man, he also dealt with practical issues, such as whether a priest should perform the Divine Liturgy once a day or more often. The great Photios writes that only one Liturgy can be celebrated by a priest on the same day, for Jesus Christ, who is our High Priest, only once suffered upon the Cross (*Ierougesen*). If a priest performs more than one Liturgy, this means that he believes that Christ suffered many times on the Cross; one crucifixion was not enough, but more were needed for our salvation. Thus, since a priest is a *typos* of Christ, he can only perform one Divine Liturgy per day.

Saint Photios also collected many maxims or aphorisms concerning daily life. Many of them were taken from the Scriptures, but some were also taken from ancient and contemporary philosophers and writers. In one of them, he writes: "To those who forget the poor and spend their time in amusements and extravagance, those who collect wealth and are greedy are unworthy of divine mercy."[16] In another maxim, he writes that it is not enough to claim physical virginity, unless the tongue, the sight, the hands, and, most importantly, the heart are virgin and clean.[17]

Unfortunately, it is not possible in such a short time to extensively present and examine Saint Photios the Great's life and writings as he was a Christian of many interests and accomplishments. It was December of 893 when the holy patriarch of Constantinople passed from this world of corruption and decay to the life of eternal glory and justification. A few days later, the church of the Imperial City received his sacred remains and paid due honor and proper tribute to one of her greatest servants in her long and saintly history. Let us finish this short homily with the conciliatory atmosphere that prevailed in Byzantium at the end of the tenth century as recorded in the Tome of Union of the Synodikon of Orthodoxy which is proclaimed in Orthodox churches every year on the Sunday of Orthodoxy:

> Eternal memory to Ignatios and Photios, the Orthodox and renowned patriarchs! Whatever has been written or said against the holy Patriarchs Germanos, Tarasios, Nikephoros, and Methodios, Ignatios, Photios, Stephen, Anthony, and Nicholas be forever Anathema, Anathema, Anathema.[18]

Notes

[1]Saint Photios, *On the Mystagogy of the Holy Spirit* (New York, 1983), p. 53.

[2]Letter 3, Ioannes Valettas, Φωτίου ʼΕπιστολαί (London, 1864), pp. 148, 154; *Mystagogy,* p. 33.

[3]Letter 2, Valettas, p. 25; *Mystagogy,* p. 35.

[4]*On the Mystagogy of the Holy Spirit,* pp. 69-70.

[5]Ibid. p. 71.

[6]Ibid. p. 46.

[7]Ibid. p. 44.

[8]Ibid.

[9]Cyril Mango, *The Homilies of Photius* . . . (Cambridge, 1958), p. 276.

[10]Ibid. p. 258.

[11]Despina S. White, *Photios* (Brookline, 1981), pp. 91-92.

[12]Mango, p. 60.

[13]Despina White and Joseph Berrigan, *The Patriarch and the Prince* (Brookline, 1982), p. 76.

[14]Mango, pp. 56-57.

[15]*Photios,* pp. 161, 164.

[16]J. Hergenrother, *Monumenta Graeca ad Photium* . . . (Regensburg, 1869), p. 26.

[17]Ibid. p. 38.

[18]Francis Dvornik, *The Photian Schism* (Cambridge, 1948), p. 434.

"The Apology" of Nestorios: A New Evaluation

It is hardly possible to represent in this short paper my conclusions on Nestorios' *Apology*. The philological and chronological problems of this book have been discussed so pertinently by Vine[1] and Abramowski[2] and they are beyond the scope of my presentation. Also M. Anastos' monograph[3] in which he sustained the position that Nestorios was Orthodox is too well known to be repeated here.

However, a careful analysis of the text of Nestorios' *Apology*, or of *The Bazaar of Heracleides*,[4] as it is also known, shows his vigorous and intense attempt to prove that he is not guilty of the heresy he was condemned for at the Third Ecumenical Council in 431. He claims that he is Orthodox in his faith and that he accepts what the Scriptures and the Fathers of the Church teach;[5] as far as the Council of Ephesos is concerned, one must remember, he says, that Meletios and Eustathios, Athanasios, and Flavian as well as Saint John Chrysostom have been condemned by Councils: "And, that I may speak briefly, Meletios and Eusthathios would not have been bishops of Antioch, if they had accepted them, nor would Athanasios be bishop of Alexandria if he were to accept the judgment of those who deprived him without hesitation and as (if it proceeded) from the orthodox. John (Chrysostom) would not be bishop of Constantinople, if he were to accept the judgment and the deprivation which was (promulgated) against him without examination as (if it proceeded) from a Council; nor again would Flavian have been bishop of Constantinople, if he were to agree to the pronouncement (proceeding) from a (ecumenical) council."[6] So he is absolutely convinced God will judge him accordingly: ". . .But I have endured the torment of my life—he writes—and all my fate in the world as the torment of one day and lo! I have now already got me/to (the time of my) dissolution, and

126

daily every day I beseech God to accomplish my dissolution, whose eyes have seen the salvation of God. . . ."[7]

It is the confession of a tortured soul. But it is also a misleading one. Nestorios was not so humble as one might think regarding these lines from his selected *Apology*. He was a proud man, too self-confident and too passionate to be considered objective and absolute sincere.

Thus a close study of Nestorios' *Apology* will show, we think, that he is neither a profound theologian nor an Orthodox one.

First of all his ideas about God are confused. Lacking the proper philosophical training he was unable to realize fully the meaning of difficult terms, as for instance, οὐσία, ὕπαρξις, ὑπόστασις, etc. A pupil of Theodore of Mopsuestia, he had not the power and the intuition to see the value of the apophatic theology of the Fathers. Thus the question of the divine οὐσία is solved by Nestorios in a simplified and unorthodox manner. For him all things have an οὐσία as the basis of their existence. God and man therefore have their own οὐσία (which, by the way, for Nestorios is identical with φύσις or nature.[8] Both the divine and the human οὐσίαι are clearly put on ontological grounds. This is of course contrary to the apophatic theology of the Fathers who are always eager to point out that the divine οὐσία is above and beyond any ontology and metaphysics. However, precisely because Nestorios has put both the divine οὐσία and the human οὐσία on the same ontological grounds, he had the fear that the *hypostatic or natural union* of Saint Cyril could mean nothing else than a union of the divine οὐσία and the human οὐσία. Now for Nestorios every οὐσία or nature is complete and independent: "For every complete nature has not need of another nature that it many be and live, in that it has in it and has received (its whole) definition that it may be."[9] Then it is obvious for him that any real union of the divine and the human οὐσία or natures is unthinkable for it would mean the change and the destruction of one of them. "For this (hypostatic union) is one that suppresses the natures, and I accept it not . . ."[10] Nestorios proclaims. Such a union is actually "a second creation"[11] "a corruptible and passible",[12] because "those which are naturally united suffer indeed in οὐσία with one another, transmitting their own sufferings of the soul and of the body . . ."[13]

Secondly, since a real union of the two οὐσίαι or natures was excluded, Nestorios was compelled to find another means by which to explain the relation of the two natures in Christ: and that was the *prosopic union*. Every οὐσία or nature according to him has its own person. No οὐσία or nature can exist without πρόσωπον[14]. This is why he speaks about the πρόσωπον *of the divinity* and the πρόσωπον *of humanity*.[15] These two persons "are thereby combined in one πρόσωπον which belongs to the two natures and to the πρόσωπον[16]. Out of this combination of the two πρόσωπα comes the πρόσωπον of union, or the common πρόσωπον of our Lord Jesus Christ.[18], or the πρόσωπον of the Messiah,[19] and the πρόσωπον of Christ.[20] or the one πρόσωπον of the two natures,[21] the πρόσωπον of the dispensation on our behalf[22], and so on. What did Nestorios really mean with this prosopic union? Contemporary scholarship still finds it difficult to ascertain and explain fully and disentangle the thread of his thought. *The Bazaar of Heracleides* was written by Nestorios in a state of deep emotionalism and confusion and his ideas are not always easy to follow. However, if one has in mind his concept on the οὐσία and the nature of divinity and the humanity, his intention emerges quite clear cut. Althought he is not sure himself how to explain this prosopic union, he positively thinks that only such a union is possible, for only such a union can preserve intact the two natures in Christ and only through this union " . . . the οὐσία of God the Word who remains eternally as he is . . . receives neither addition or diminution . . ."[23], "the οὐσίαι remain without change . . ."[24] "and avoid any kind of mixture and confusion.[25]

There is no doubt that such kind of union sounds reasonable and consistent with Nestorios' shallow philosophical system. But it can hardly be in agreement with the whole scheme of the Orthodox soteriology. For the prosopic union is not in reality a full union of the divine and human but rather a *point of contact*, an external mark upon which the external characteristics or the properties and the qualities can meet or can concur.[26] Here we actually have a περιχώρησις or an ἀντίδοσις restricted between the two persons in Christ and not ἀντίδοσις τῶν ἰδιωμάτων of the two natures in Christ.[27] Soteriologically speaking such a stand can have grave repercussions for the redemption of mankind, because this Nestorian distinction of the natures, united only in their respective persons, excludes the deification of man in Christ and in him the whole mankind. We can then justly claim here that the whole Nestorian concept of the salvation of mankind is rather weak, deficient and one-sided.[28] This also can be seen in his strange concept of the ransom Christ paid for us to Satan,[29] in his theory of the moral progress of the human nature of Christ,[30] and in his notion that Christ offered his sacrifice on the Cross even for himself.[31] Thus the man-Christ related externally with God the Word is still more than evident in the *Bazaar*. Moreover, Nestorios' teaching on the eucharist is alien to the tradition of the Church. Already before his condemnation Nestorios claimed that we neither eat nor drink the divinity of Christ in the sacrament of the eucharist.[32] In the *Bazaar* he follows the same line of thought adding that in the eucharist the bread remains bread and "the bread is the body (of Christ) by faith and not by nature . . ."[33] Therefore he dismisses the real change of the elements of the bread and the wine into the body and blood of Christ.[34] In addition, not only the bread is simply by faith the body of Christ, but it is *only* the body of Christ, that is, only his human nature.[35] Thus the distinction of the two natures in Christ becomes apparent in the sacrament of the eucharist itself. This distinction is carried by Nestorios in the whole system of his liturgical theology in which he introduces the adoration due to the person of union, thus excluding the real adoration due to the human nature of Christ. In other words, according to Nestorios the adoration due to the human nature of Christ does not take place with full right because it is the deified flesh of the Lord and the Word of God, but any honour or adoration due to the human nature of Christ is given simply because of the prosopic union or because of the common πρόσωπον of the union. Such a notion could lead to anthropology, as Saint Cyril soon acknowledged, and could strip the whole liturgical theology of the Church of its profound mystical and theocentric meaning.

The *Bazaar of Heracleides* includes a great amount of material for long and pertinent discussion concerning Nestorios' teaching and interpretation and controversial theological problems. To do justice to Nestorios we must accept the fact that in his *Bazaar* he took for some serious steps towards the tradition of the Church. No serious student of Nestorios could rightly claim today that in his *Bazaar* he continued to adhere to the concept of συνάφεια that is to the association or conjuction of the two natures in Christ in the sense of association in distance or separation in space. We must also take seriously his disclaimer that he introduced two Christs or two Sons in his christological teaching.[37] It appears also that in the *Bazaar* he made the attempt to dissociate himself from the theory of the two separated adorations due to Christ.[38] It appears appropriate to acknowledge Nestorios' good intentions on the controversy regarding the names and titles of the Virgin Mary (Christotokos or Theotokos?) although we must stress his inability to grasp the real essence of the controversy. He was unable to perceive that behind this controversy the whole scheme of the Orthodox Christology and the Orthodox soteriology was at stake. He failed to realize that his theology was building up a wall of partition between God and man, an everlasting division between divine and human, the dimness of any hope that man can become divine. Nestorios in the last analysis failed to understand that the Word of God "was made man that we might be made God."[40] Here lies the great responsibility of Nestorios, that is in his complete failure to see that behind the christological controversy of his times the whole theology of the Church on the redemption of mankind could stand or fall.

Thus in view of the evidence accumulated in the *Bazaar* the suggestion that if Nestorios were present in the Council of Chalcedon (451), he would become a pillar of Orthodoxy,[41] is a sheer conjecture.

Notes

[1] A. R. Vine, *An Approach to Christology. The Bazaar of Heracleides* (London 1948).

[2] L. Abramowski, *Untersuchungen zum literarischen Nachass des Nestorios* (Bonn 1956). Also: "Untersuchungen zum Liber Heraclidis des Nestorius," in *Corpus Scriptorum Christianorum Orientalium,* vol. 242, tome 22 (Louvain 1963).

[3] M. Anastos, "Nestorios was Orthodox," *The Dumbarton Oaks Papers* 16 (1962) 119-40.

[4] For the English translation of the text see: Nestorius, *The Bazaar of Heraclides,* translated from the Syriac and edited with an Introduction, Notes and Appendices by G. R. Driver and L. Hodgson (Oxford 1925). For a fuller discussion on the Bazaar and Nestorius' theology in general see my book: *Συμβολαὶ εἰς τὴν περὶ τοῦ Νεστορίου ἔρευναν* (Athens, 1964). For reviews of my books see Prof. John Karmires' review in *The Greek Orthodox Theological Review* 12 (1966/67) 212-15 and Father D.J. Chitty's review in *Theology,* 70 (1967) 367-68.

[5] Bazaar of Heracleides, pp. 94-95, 154, 228, 255, 378.

[6] Ibid. p. 377.

[7] Ibid. p. 379.

[8] Ibid., p. 138, 145, 153-54, 159, 166, 170, 193, 200-01, 217, 219, 227, 230-31, 233, 245, 247, 255, 294, 299, 313, 316, 324, 326-27.

[9] Ibid. p. 304.

[10] Ibid. p. 161.

[11] Ibid. p. 36, 39, 161.

[12] Ibid. p. 163.

[13] Ibid. p. 179.

[14] Ibid. pp. 218-19, 247.

[15] Ibid. p. 207.

[16] Ibid. p. 246.

[17] Ibid. pp. 143, 144, 152, 153, 158, 166, 182, 219, 241, 247, 262.

[18] Ibid. pp. 171, 172, 149, 146, 318, 319.

[19] Ibid., p. 143.

[20] Ibid. p. 168.

[21] Ibid. pp. 58, 146, 148, 163, 196, 216, 218, 161, 167, 219, 319.

[22] Ibid. pp. 171, 172, 219, 301.

[23] Ibid. p. 144.

[24]Ibid. p. 23.

[25]Ibid. pp. 26-27.

[26]Ibid. p. 166-67.

[27]In contrast to Nestorios' "antidosis" of persons, Saint John Damascus writes: "And this is the manner of the mutual communication, either nature giving in exchange to the other its own properties through the identity of the subsistence and the interpenetration of the parts with one another," *Exposition of the Orthodox Faith,* 4. The English translation in: *A Select Library of Nicene and Post-Nicene Fathers of the Christian Church,* Vol. 9, (Grand Rapids, 1955), p. 49.

[28]See in my book on Nestorios, pp. 210ff. A Harnack has already made the comment that "The Christology of the Antiochians was therefore not soteriologically determined," *History of Dogma,* Vol. 4 (London 1898), 166. R.V. Sellers on the other hand, although he finds the Antiochians are indeed interested in soteriology, is, none the less, forced to accept that their soteriology "is not fully developed." See his *Two Ancient Christologies"* (London, 1954), pp. 117, 129, 142, 184.

[29]*Bazaar of Heracleides,* p. 73.

[30]Ibid. pp. 44ff., 66ff., 81, 84, 91, 200, 206, 230-31, 248, 237, 255, 261. See also pp. 213, 240, 243, 245-46, 249.

[31]Ibid. pp. 250-51.

[32]F. Loofs, *Nestoriana* (Halle, 1905), 227-28. On the repercussion of Nestorios' Christology on the Eucharist see: H. Chadwick, *Eucharist and Christology in the Nestorian Controversy," Journal of Theological Studies,* 2, (1951), p. 145-64. See also Paul Tillich, *A History of Christian Thought,* Ed. P.H. John, 1956), 73, 77.

[33]*Bazaar of Heracleides,* pp. 29-30, 32, 55, 327-28.

[34]Ibid. pp. 32-33 and 327-28.

[35]Ibid. pp. 31-33.

[36]Ibid. pp. 210, 313, 314.

[37]Ibid. pp. 66, 151, 158-59, 174, 206, 225, 235, 300, 302, 315, 317, 388-89.

[38]Ibid. pp. 221, 226, 228, 236, 238-39, 313, 395.

[39]V. Lossky, *The Mystical Theology of the Eastern Church,* (London 1957), 10.

[40]Saint Athanasios, *On the Incarnation of the Word* 54. The Library of Christian Classics, vol. 3. *Christology of the Later Fathers* (Philadelphia, 1954), p. 107.

[41]F. Loofs, *Nestorius and his Place in the History of Christian Doctrine* (Cambridge 1914), p. 21. George Davis Mooken, *A Re-Examination of the Theology of Nestorius. A thesis submitted to Leonard Theological College* (Jabalpur 1961), 13.

Saint Nikodemos the Hagiorite

On 31 May 1955, the Holy Synod of the Eccumenical Patriarchate of Constantinople, with Patriarch Athenagoras presiding, approved and signed a "Synodical Act" on Saint Nikodemos the Hagiorite. This "Synodical Act" stated that through the guidance of the Holy Spirit and the proper synodical deliberations, the Holy Synod decreed that Saint Nikodemos the Hagiorite be enumerated among the saints of the Church and be honored with special services, hymns, and 'encomia' on the fourteenth of July, the day of his passing from this world to everlasting life.[1]

The "Synodical Act" of the Ecumenical Patriarchate of Constantinople was decreed in response to an official report and request submitted by the "geron," the abbot, of the monastic community of Mount Athos. Geron Ananias expressed the unanimous consent of the monks of Mount Athos, and without any doubt, the enthusiastic agreement of the Orthodox Church, regarding the "sainthood" of Saint Nikodemos. Thus the "Synodical Act" based on the universally recognized holiness of the life of Saint Nikodemos, on the concrete facts that Saint Nikodemos had lived a life according to Christ, a life in which he had been a living image of virtue; moreover he had proved himself to be a teacher of the Church through the numerous writings which he wrote for the spiritual benefit, uplifting, and guidance of the Christian people.[2]

It was a recognition and an honor already overdue. The monks of Mount Athos call Saint Nikodemos "the greatest post-Byzantine figure in Orthodox theology."[3] Elias Lavriotis, the First Secretary of the Monastic Community of Mount Athos wrote that the monks of Mount

132

Athos and all the Orthodox people consider Saint Nikodemos as a true saint, a great theologian, a man of great humility, and a holy man who led a life equal to the angels, a truly apostolic life. Because of his exemplary life and his immense and profound theological knowledge, he greatly contributed toward the correct understanding and solution of the staggering problems of his times. Thus he armed the Greek nation spiritually, morally, and religiously and prepared the Greek Orthodox people for their struggle of liberation in 1821. "He has been the binding link between the fallen religious Byzantium and the rising soul of Hellenism."[14]

Theokletos Dionysiates, another great monk of Mount Athos, wrote:

> No one can contest the fact that Saint Nikodemos lived the Orthodox spirit of the Fathers in all its facets. He condensed in himself all their divinely-inspired wisdom and experience. His holy soul moved towards all the immeasurable extensions of the Holy Spirit. And he participated, as the Fathers did, in the wisdom and in the knowledge of God, 'through sufferings' . . . Nikodemos was a true man and a true Christian . . . [5]

Non-Orthodox scholars call him a man in whom the Greek Church is again glorified,[6] and there is no doubt that in the person of Saint Nikodemos the Orthodox Church has found all the spiritual brilliance and all the "theological intensity" of a trully great Father and Teacher. For this reason most of his work have been published again and again during this century and the biographies written by the celebrated Athonite monk Theokletos Dionysiates[7] and Dr. Constantine Cavarnos[8] are already out of print.

Nikodemos was born in 1749 on the island of Naxos, one of the islands of the Kyklades. His baptismal name was Nicholas and his last name Kallivourtsis. His parents, Anthony and Anastasia, were very pious people. In fact, his mother later became a nun at the Convent of Saint John Chrysostom in Naxos and was renamed Agathe. From his early years young Nicholas was distinguished by his exceptional alertness, his absolute devotion to sacred as well as to secular learning. He was gifted "with great acuteness of mind, accurate perception, intellectual brightness" and with a vast, photographic, and creative memory.[9] In a letter one of his fellow-students calls young Nickolas "an excellent miracle of his time."[10] "He knew by memory everything he read, not only the philosophical, economic, medical, astronomic, and military treatises, but also all the ancient and new poets and historians. Greek and Latin, as well as all the writings of the Holy Fathers. He could read a book once and he could remember it throughout his whole life . . ."[11]

His first teacher in Naxos was the wise and prudent Archimandrite Chrysanthos, the brother of the neomartyr and the apostle of the Greek nation, Saint Kosmas Aitolos.

Since Naxos could not offer enough for the impatient and already rising young scholar and theologian, Nicholas was sent to Smyrna. There he studied under the guidance of the famous master of his times Ierotheos Voulismas at he renowned "Evangelike Schole." Nikodemos stayed in Smyrna for a period of five years. His brilliant mind soon attracted the admiration of all and he becames the teacher of his fellow students. Meanwhile, he mastered besides the Greek language, Latin, Italian, and French.

The persecution and the massacre of the Christians by the Turks in Smyrna forced young Nickolas to return to his native Naxos, where he became the secretary to Metropolitan Anthimos Vardis. Here he met the highly admired and respected priest-monks Gregory and Niphon and the monk Arsenios, all of whom werre well versed in the Athonitic way of life an practitioners of the spiritual 'art' of hesychasm. Their moral excellence and their true piety influenced Nicholas immensely. They introduced him to the life of he ascetics of Mount Athos and persuaded him to follow the life of the Spirit, the life of unceasing prayer, the life of hesychasm, poverty, humility, and absolute devotion to Christ.

But the man who influenced Nicholas the most was Saint Makarios Notaras, Metropolitan of Corinth,[12] one of the greatest spiritual leaders of his time renowned as a pastoral teacher of exceptional depth and wise vision. Young Nicholas visited Metropolitan Makarios on the island of Hydra and soon they become close friends and spiritual brothers united by a truly deep spiritual bond. In Hydra, Nicholas met another great monk, Silvestros of Caesarea, who cultivated in the youthful heart of Nicholas the burning longing for the blessed life of contemplation. Thus in 1755, with the recommendation letters of Silvestros, Nicholas left Naxos for the Holy Mountain. There he renounced the world and was tonsured a monk, receiving the "small habit" and the name Nikodemos. The holy fathers of the Monastery of Dionysiou then appointed him reader of their cenobitic community.[13]

Reading, writing, and teaching were his daily occupations. His mind, his hand, and his pen were used for he propagation of the word of God. He continuously studied the books and the manuscripts kept in the libraries of Mount Athos. Even today one can read the notations which Nikodemos himself made on many manuscripts on the Holy Mountain. For instance, in a codex of the fifteenth century containing the works of

Dionysios the Areopagite, one can read the following comment: "I read this glorious book full of the sacred mystical dogmas of the Holy Spirit and the benefit I derived was more than great."[14] While thus engrossed in his studies and writing, he also had to find a means to secure his living. He copied manuscripts, as he himself writes, and led "the life of a worker and laborer: digging, sowing, harvesting . . ."[15] But his heart, full of humility, was burning with the holy fire of an Apostle.

Saint Nikodemos did not always stay at the same monastery. He stayed in the beginning at the Monastery of Dionysiou, then at the Kelli of the Skourdaioi brothers, then in the Skete of the Pantokrator. He even travelled and stayed on the small island of Skyropoula across Euboia, where he practiced a strict ascetic life. Then again he lived in a small and quiet *kalyva* on Mount Athos with the support of the Skourtaioi brothers. There he lived the life of a poor worker and laborer. His diet, according to his spiritual brother Euthymios (*paradelphos*), consisted of rice boiled in water, honey diluted in water, olives, soaked fava beans, and bread. He rarely used to eat fish. Those who lived with him and knew him say that he lived the life of an angel. He was humble, sweet, meek, and without possessions. Whenever he spoke of himself he would say, "I am a monster," "I am a dead dog." "I am a nonentity," "unwise," "uneducated."[16] Because he lived in many monasteries and he enjoyed the affection of most of the monks, he became during his life after his death a universally accepted and recognized representative of the tradition, the teaching, and the ascetic life of Mount Athos. Hence he was called Saint Nikodemos the Hagiorite.

He died at the age of sixty. The hard way of life, his poor diet, and his hard and exhausting labors weakened his frail body and he fell ill. He felt that the end was coming. He confessed, received holy unction, and partook of the holy eucharist. He was continuously praying with his lips, since he was unable to practice the mental prayer. He received once more the holy eucharist, he crossed his hands, and stretched out his legs. He was now in full spiritual tranquility. "Teacher, are you resting?" his brothers asked. He replied, "I have placed Christ within me, how it is possible for me not to be Creator. He was buried at the kelli of Skourdaioi and his precious head is still kept there.

A glimpse at the list of his writings will immediately reveal that he was indeed a prolific writer of wide interest. There is no aspect of theology which was unknown to him. His writings cover all the fields of theology. The Old and the New Testaments, dogma, the liturgical life of the church, the canons, and the field of pastoral care attracted the attention of this great monk.

Moreover, he also composed hymns for the Church. He wrote both *idiomela* and *prosomoia.* He believed very strongly in the importance of chanting and he used to say: "When you hear the sacred chanting in the church, especially on holy days, grace acts within you and causes spiritual sweetness."[18] Furthermore, he advised: "Psalmodize in your heart the spiritual songs of the church at your home, at the market-place, where you work, where you walk, and everywhere else."[19]

He compiled and edited an anthology of Psalms, and later he translated into modern Greek the text of the Psalms edited by Euthymios Zygavenos. The comments and the footnotes of Saint Nikodemos cover almost half of this publication. This work shows Saint Nikodemos' assimilation of the message and poetic beauty of the Psalms. In fact, it seems likely that he had a mastery of the Hebrew language.[20]

Then he published in the spoken Greek of his time the exegetical work *The Fourteen Epistles of Saint Paul* by Theophylaktos, the archbishop of Bulgaria during the eleventh century, as well as the seven Catholic Epistles. Realizing the spiritual value of these commentaries and the lack of any contemporary text, Nikodemos undertook this work of translation. Two points should be noted. First of all, Nikodemos humbly calls himself 'translator' (*metaphrastes*), although he contributed heavily to these publications with his own personal comments. Secondly, Saint Nikodemos was a man of the Bible. Not only did he know, study, and write commentaries on the Holy Scripture, but he was also fully aware of the unquestionable and unequivocal position of Scripture in the framework of Orthodox dogma and practice. With his own example he refuted the accusation that Orthodox theologians are 'unbiblical,' or that they fail to grasp the importance of Scripture in the formation of dogma and in the practice of the Orthodox way of life. Saint Nikodemos writes: "Divine Scripture is the divine science that makes us more educated than all the philosophers, more wise than all the moralists and political theorists; and it alone transforms us from carnal, natural, and wretched into holy, spiritual and blessed (men)."[21] He continues: "In Divine Scripture is found the highest truth that illuminates the mind which has truth as its natural object, because the words of Scriptures are the words of God, of the Holy Spirit, that is, of truth itself and of grace itself."[22] He also especially stresses the pedagogical value of Saint Paul's letters: "You must always read . . . the venerable Epistles of Paul, in order to learn from them the dogmas of the Orthodox faith, the traditions of the holy Apostles, the duties of the Christian life and also how to avoid the vices and acquire the Christian virtues."[23] In truth, Saint Nikodemos was a man of "Pauline love."[24]

As a great patristic scholar, he excelled in the study of the lives and writings of the Fathers; he was immersed in the spirit of the Fathers and was continuously rejoicing in the "spiritual gardens" of patristic life and thought.

> Along with the Scriptures, read also the divine Fathers, the interpreters of the Scriptures. You will derive no less pleasure from them than from the Scriptures, for by developing through their sacred writings the hidden meanings contained in the Scriptures, the Fathers enlighten the mind and enable it to know things it did not know before . . . Ineffable delight and joy shall be produced in your soul from the interpretations and words of the divine Fathers, so that you too will cry out those enthusiastic words of David, saying: 'I have delighted in the way of thy testimonies, as much as in all riches' (Ps 118.14).[25]

The lives of the Fathers and their writings bear witness to "a practical faith rather than a theoretical faith."[26] It is spiritual exercise of our Fathers who have fallen asleep and of those who are still living. We must follow their footsteps in teacing, in behavior, in forbearance, in love, in patience, in persecutions, and in sufferings. We must never separate ourselves from the Fathers neither in this world nor in the future one.[27] Saint Nikodemos followed the Fathers throughout his life and all his works are replate with quotations from them. A quick glimpse at his beautiful book *Nea Klimax* (or New Ladder) will prove this point.

But Saint Nikodemos' great contribution to the field of patrology was his celebrated edition of the *Philokalia*. Under the influence, instructions, and help of his great friend and mentor Saint Makarios, the metropolitan of Corinth,[28] he prepared his carefully done and indeed splendid collection from the lives and the sayings of the great ascetic or 'neptic' Fathers, such as Saint Anthony the Great, Saint Mark the Ascetic, Abba Evagrios, Saint Maximos the Confessor.[29] The work emphasizes the recapturing and reliving of the *noera proseuche*, the prayer in the mind. Monks, parish clergy, and laymen can, by praying in this way, liberate themselves from the trivialities of this world and thus live the life of *theosis* through the energies and the illumination of the Holy Spirit. "This mental prayer is the light which illumines man's soul and inflames his heart with the fire of love of God. It is the chain linking God with man and man with God."[30] The impact of his edition of the *Philokalia* can be understood from the fact that it was translated almost immediately into Slavonic by Paissy Velichkovsky, upon which the contemporary English translations are mostly based.

Of great patristic value are also the following works of Saint
Nikodemos: *Evergetinos,* the *Works of Saint Symeon the New
Theologian,*and the *Works of Saint Gregory Palamas.* In the
Evergetinos.[31] Saint Nikodemos published a collection of saying of the
"God-bearing Fathers" where he emphasizes their spiritual struggles
in order to overcome human and spiritual weakness and to become completely *apatheis,* free from all the passions of soul and body. The publication of the *Works of Saint Symeon the New Theologian* is one of the
most valuable contributions of Saint Nikodemos to patristic studies. Saint
Nikodemos not only preserved for us the precious texts of Saint Symeon,
but also drew the attention of his generation and all generations to come
to the importance of the Holy Spirit in the life of the true Christian.

Saint Nikodemos prepared the manuscript of the works of Saint
Greogory Palamas and sent it to Vienna for publication. Unfortunately,
for reasons not very clear, the manuscripts disappeared. His introduction has survived, however, and in it can be seen Saint Nikodemos' great
admiration for the Fathers of the Church and his devotion to the Orthodox Sinaitic and Hagioritic tradition.[32]

Among the famous mustical and spiritual writings of Saint Nikodemos
is *Unseen Warfare.* This is actually an adaptation of *Spiritual Combat,*
written by the Italian priest Lorenzo Scupoli (c. 1530-1610).[33] He also
adapted *The Spiritual Exercises,* written by Giovani P. Pinamonti
(1632-1703). Although Saint Nikodemos was accused of plagiarism in
publishing these adaptations, he always cited the original sources of his
works. Moreover, he never failed to adapt the non-Orthodox books to
the spirit of Orthodoxy, by stressing Orthodox doctrine and the practice
of hesychasm and by removing alien influences such as the doctrine of
Purgatory and the cult of the Sacred Heart. In his work *The Pedalion*
(Rudder), which places Saint Nikodemos among the greatest canonists
of the Church, the holy canons are codified. In addition, interpretation
and commentary which express the eternal spirit of the Orthodox theology
and practice are provided. Saint Nikodemos used the 'demotic' dialect,
so that the holy canons could be easily read by Christians of all walks
of life. In his commentaries Saint Nikodemos showed how theology and
praxis in Orthodoxy go together. Theology, doctrine, ethics, liturgics,
and canon law are all part of one entity, the living experience of the
Church. Saint Nikodemos brought together and united the past with the
present, projecting them to the coming future with extraordinary vision.
Perhaps some of his comments and interpretations sound out of date
today, since the Church is not static. In fact, the term *pedalion* means
and implies movement, new situations, new problems. Christ, the captain

of the ship, is at the rudder, ready to lead the ship, the Church, to the safe port of salvation.

> And indeed (Saint Nikodemos writes to his readers) this canonical handbook is a sort of rudder and spiritual compass; since it alone, in truth, points accurately and undeviatingly to the pole — that is to say, to Heaven itself. With it, as with a rudder, the Church of Christ can very surely and very safely steer her course on her voyage to the really calm harbor of that blissful and wantless destination.[34]

In fact, Saint Nikodemos says that the Holy Spirit is the constructor of this rudder.[35] Where the Holy Spirit breathes there is freedom. Some 'scholars' considered the *Rudder* as inflexible and out of reality. But Saint Nikodemos was a practical man and would unboudtedly assert that the canons were made for the Church and not the Church for the canons.

His *Christoetheia, The Garden of Graces, The New Ladder,* and *the Spiritual Exercises* make Saint Nikodemos a great "moralist." But he was not a moralist for the sake of morality. He was a man of God. The most important imperative of the Christian way of life is obedience to the will of God and a total embracement of the cross of Christ, so that the Christians would be ready to die rather than violate the will of God. True morality is an absolute identification with the will of God, to offer one's freedom to the freedom of God, to attempt to lead the life of perfection.[36] Saint Nikodemos declares that the moral value of a Christian is not soft and easy. It is the virtue of a brave and magnanimous soldier, who must always fight against the vices, sorrows, and temptations which are created by the demons, by his fellowmen, or even by his own corrupted nature. Only with "spiritual arms" can one fight all the vicissitudes of life.[37] And what is the goal? Paradise. And paradise is the company and the joy of being close to Christ, the Holy Mother of God, the angels, and all the saints.[38]

The liturgical and practical interests of Saint Nikodemos were extensive. The *Euchologion,* the *Synaxaristes,* the *Manual of Confession,* the *New Theotokarion, The New Martyrologion,* and his book *On the New Continual Communion of the Divine Mysteries* show how he deeply loved and lived the liturgical life of the Church. His interest in the saints was great since he believed together with Saint John Chrysostom (1st Homily on Saint Babylas) that the grace of the Holy Spirit is in the naked body and the remains of the martyrs and saints. Moreover, he agrees with Saint Gregory Palamas that just as the divinity of Christ was not separated from his holy body during the three days of his stay in Hades, in the same way the grace of God has not been separated from the remains of the saints and martyrs.[39]

The authorship of the work *On the Continual Communion of the Divine Mysteries* has been contested many times. No one can be sure, but in all probability it was written by an Athonite monk, was corrected and amplified by Saint Nikodemos, and was published by Saint Makarios of Corinth.[40] There is no doubt that it expresses the mind of Saint Nikodemos, who was appalled that even the monks of Mount Athos would receive holy Communion only three times every year. In the book, the author demonstrates the need for frequent participation in holy Communion with convincing arguments from the canons and the holy Fathers. Holy Communion warms the coolness and the indifference of the soul and strenghtens it: helps the spiritual growth (*prokope*) of those who live according to Christ, and cleanses and sanctifies their souls, bringing "spiritual health" and salvation.[41] Naturally, the author of the book presupposes the necessary preparation for receiving Holy Communion.[42] One can imagine Saint Nikodemos' indignation and anger when the Ecumenical Patriarch Prokopios condemned 'synodically' the book and its author. But the mind of the Church has won over the opinion of even an ecumenical patriarch and the influence of this small book was greatly felt and is still felt in the life of the Church.

Was Saint Nikodemos interested in the dogmas of the Church? His books *Confession of Faith* and his *Apology* show how deeply he was immersed in Orthodox theology. But one thing was clear for Saint Nikodemos: he never separated doctrine from the spiritual and practical life of the people of God. Thus he was an all-around theologian, a man of faith, a man of action, and a man of *hesychia*, of spiritual "quietness" which leads to the participation of the divine energies of God.

Runciman writes that Saint Nikodemos cannot be rated highly as a scholarly editor or textual critic. But he adds that his compilation of the *Philokalia* is of great importance not only because it includes many unpublished and some otherwise unknown texts, but also because it shows the continuity of the Christian mystical thought. "And mystical experience," Runciman concludes, "lies at the heart of Orthodoxy."[43]

Indeed, Saint Nikodemos used to write from his exceptionally photographic and creative memory. Mistakes could be made. His admirable memory was both an asset and sometimes a handicap for deriving and verifying precise information. However, Saint Nikodemos wrote or published more than one hundred works. Behind his vast amount of knowledge, one cannot but recognize the great scholar and the superb thinker. He was thinking, praying, and writing. He wrote for both the educated and the uneducated. "I must help and benefit my educated brother as well as the simple brother," he wrote.[44] He stood firmly on the concrete and unshakeable grounds of tradition. He believed that "the holy synods and the divine Fathers did not utter words of their own, nor did they speak with the spirit of this world, as do wordly men, but they spoke with the illumination and grace of the Holy Spirit, and their words are divine teachings that lead men to the kingdom of God."[45]

Saint Nikodemos is not a humanist, but rather a traditionalist in the sense that "the mind is an image of God" and therefore "the more the loving mind ascends to its beloved God through the contemplation of his divine perfections, the more God who is loved condescends from his height toward the loving, and becomes united with it, deifies it, and fills it with gifts."[46] Greek humanists influenced by the European humanism of their times, like Athanasios Psalides, Lambros Photiades, Eugenios Voulgaris, and Adamantios Koraes are not of his kind. He follows the line of Athanasios Parios, Makarios Notaras, and Kosmas Aitolos. For these holy men, European humanism was based and developed on the humanistic concepts of self-reliance and self-efficiency of man. This is a Pelagian heresy and at the heart of the matter a sheer Nestorianism.[47] This does not mean that Saint Nikodemos was unfamiliar with the sciences of his time. Not at all. He was well-versed in ancient Greek philosophy, and in the achievements of the sciences of his times.

Did Nikodemos have a full and clear understanding of the tragic conditions of his nation? It is true that Saint Nikodemos did not arm himself with arms to fight the oppressors of his people. He did not leave the boundaries of Mount Athos to preach.[48] But he must be seen as a monk devoted to his Lord and endowed with the *charisma* to write. He knew very well that the freedom of his nation depended upon its liberation from the spiritual bondage which undermined the spiritual foundations of the nation. His writings had the purpose of preparing his people for the time of liberation.[49] In his *Neon Martyrologion* can be seen his profound and sincere concern for the oppression of his nation. Most of the martyrs which he presents suffered martyrdom because they refused to subjugate themselves to the will of the conqueror. He speaks about: the "the yoke of bondage" the "Agarens," the "tyrants," the "Turks" and "Mohammed." *Allaxopistia* change from the Orthodox Christian faith to the Moslem religion, is considered a grave sin by Saint Nikodemos.[50] Orthodoxy was the strengthening weapon which gave the hope for the coming resurrection of the nation to the oppressed. From that historical vista, Saint Nikodemos fulfilled his duty to the utmost of his abilities.

Saint Nikodemos' life is associated with the *Kollyvades* movement.

This movement arose in 1754 as a reaction to the monks of the skete of Saint Anne who decided to perform the memorial services for the dead on Sundays. The monks initiated this change because they were involved with building a church with the financial assistance of Orthodox Christians from all over the Balkan peninsula and especially from Smyrna. Since they were busy and tired from the labors of the week, they held the memorial services for the dead during the Sunday vigil services. This innovation created commotion on Mount Athos and the monks as well as the laymen were divided into two parties. Among the *Kollyvades* who opposed this new practice were men like Saint Nikodemos, Saint Makarios of Corinth, Christophoros of Arta, Agapios of Kypros, Athanasios of Paros and Neophytos of Kausokalyvites. Among the supporters of the new practice were learned men such as the monk Theodoretos of Ioannina, Vessarion of Rapsanes, and others.

The *Kollyvades* argued that Sunday was the day of the Lord's resurrection and therefore memorial services for all the departed could not take place. On the other hand, *Kollyvades* were accused of moving the Divine Liturgy to the pre-dawn hours and of celebrating the Presanctified Liturgy after sunset. Saint Nikodemos argued in his *Pedalion* that indeed the Liturgy of the Presanctified gifts should be celebrated during the afternoon hours. In addition, the teaching of the *Kollyvades* on the need for frequent communion was mistakenly understood to mean the elimination of the necessary preparation (fasting and confession), which was, of course, not true. The *Kollyvades* were also accused of reading all the prayers of the Liturgy aloud.

The *Kollyvades,* who were not the majority on Mount Athos, did not accept these accusations. They always claimed that they followed and observed the liturgical traditions and practices of the Church. Saint Nikodemos, in his writings and especially in his *Pedalion,* asserted that he followed the true *praxis* of the early liturgical life of the Church and insisted that Sunday is of greater importance than Saturday. In any event, in 1772, Patriarch Theodosios II of Constantinople, together with the consent of Sophronios, the Patriarch of Jerusalem, decreed that to sing memorial services on Saturday is not contrary to the doctrines of the Church and to perform these memorial services on Sunday does not constitute a sin.[51]

One can understand the sorrow and the anguish of Saint Nikodemos. He was even accused of being a heretic! But his profound religious experience and his love for *hesychia,* the inner tranquility of the heart which led him constantly toward God, sustained him.

Saint Nikodemos considered sin as the greatest failure of man because with sin man fails to achieve the ultimate end and goal of he life for which he was created. He writes that "the greatest and most perfect achievement that man can think of is to approach God and be united with Him."[52] For Saint Nikodemos *theosis* is the transcendent state and perfection of the mind. "Eternal, therefore, the Holy spirit," he writes, "in whom lies every *theosis* to deify you and make you god by grace. Know that if your mind is not deified by the Holy Spirit, it is impossible for you to be saved."[53]

Saint Nikodemos considered prayer the greatest virtue of all. He especially treasured the 'Jesus Prayer': "Lord Jesus Christ, Son of God, have mercy upon me."[54] According to the Fathers, especially those who are called 'wakeful' (*neptikoi*), this short prayer is the prayer of the mind and of the heart and consists chiefly of gathering the mind into the heart without uttering a word, but only discursive reason which speaks in the heart. This brief prayer is repeated with controlled breathing.[55] Saint Nikodemos mentions the spiritual value of this prayer. He writes: "Many great gifts result from this holy interior prayer. These are enumerated by the God-inspired Fathers who are called 'wakeful.' I shall mention here only the most general one, which begets the other gifts: becoming a likeness of God and attaining union with him."[56] Moreover, this prayer "unites the mind with God, who is above all creatures. It purifies, illumines, and perfects the mind more than all the algebras, physics, metaphysics, and all the other sciences of external philosophy."[57]

Saint Nikodemos knew well the paramount importance of the Holy Spirit in the spiritual advancement and perfection of a Christian. Only life in and through the Holy Spirit makes man's existence worthy of union with God.[58] He writes:

If you desire to acquire the gifts of the Holy Spirit, first cleanse your heart of passions and the predispositions of sin, and make it a temple and dwelling-place worthy of being inhabited by the Holy Spirit. How? Through inner attention and the return of the mind to the heart. Then practice sacred mental prayer in the heart saying, 'Lord Jesus Christ, Son of God, have mercy upon me.' When you prepare your heart, my beloved then the all-holy, all-good, and most man-loving Spirit comes and dwells in you perceptibly, actively, manifestly. Then, my brother, you will receive from the Holy Spirit whatever you long for. Do you love the gift of wisdom? You will receive it. Do you want to partake of he gift of the Apostles? You will acquire it. Do you aspire after the gift of martyrdom? You will receive it, if it is to your interest. Do you love joy? Do you love faith?

Do you love love? Do you love the gifts of discernment (*diakrisis*), insight (*diorasis*), foreknowledge (*proorasis*, prophecy? The Holy Spirit will give you all these things.[59]

This is a basic prerequisite for receiving these beautiful gifts of the Holy Spirit. One must love the Holy Spirit; all these will be given, Saint Nikodemos writes, "if you love the Holy Spirit with all the power of your soul, and if you have him always without an interruption, deep in your memory and in your heart."[60]

This emphasis by Saint Nikodemos on the life of *hesychia* or mental-prayer and on the life of the Spirit in general, does not make him alien to the problems of his times or indifferent to the earthly obstacles and difficulties of daily life. As we have already seen, he was both a man of theory and a man of practice. His care for both the erudite and the simple and his interest in the application of 'strictness' (*akriveia*) and 'leniency' (*oikonomia*) prove how sensitive he was to the problems which the common man and woman face in their daily lives.[61] The topics of his *Chrestoetheia* (Christian morality) show how broad were his interests and how much he really knew the weaknesses and the pitfalls of human nature. He writes about the dances of his days, the problem of drunkenness, the dangers arising from playing cards, and the satanic form and meaning of sorcery.[62] With affection and humility he advises the Christians to go to church frequently, to wash their hands beforehand, and to care equally for both their physical and spiritual needs.[63] Moreover, he encourages the workers, farmers, shoe-makers, and tailors to honor their art (*techne*) with dignity, sincerity, and justice.[64]

He speaks to the heart concerning the great value of the 'extended family' and how profitable, spiritually, morally, and even financially, it is for a family to live together in the same home with the grand-parents, and the uncles and aunts.[65]

With the sharpened eye of the good psychologist, he advises every Christian:

> So stand always on guard in fear and trembling, fearing more for yourself than for others. And be assured that every good word you may utter to your neighbor and every rejoicing for his sake is the action and the fruit of the Holy Spirit in you, whereas every bad word and scornful condemnation comes from your evil nature and suggestions of the devil.[66]

Then he proceeds with the observation:

. . .when you judge severely some wrong action of your neighbor, you must know that a small root of the same wickedness is also in your own heart, which, by its passionate nature, teaches you to make suppositions about others and to judge them . . . But an eye that is pure and without passion looks too without passion on the actions of others, and not with evil.[67]

This is the spirit, the compassion, and the genuine love of a true Christian. Saint Nikodemos was just that. Indeed he was a saint!

In the *Apolytikion* or dismissal hymn which is sung when the Church commemorates Saint Nikodemos, this great monk and spiritual father is called "light of the world." His vast knowledge of the Scriptures and of the Fathers, his exemplary life, his profound sense of devotion and duty to the Church and to his brothers and sisters in Christ, and his balanced vision of contemplation and action make him one of the greatest teachers and Fathers of the Church. His impact on the spiritual life of the Eastern Orthodox Church through his spiritual writings and life is deeply felt in the hearts and minds of the Orthodox people. Thus the faithful of the Church cherish his wisdom, his faith, and his absolute and ultimate surrender to the radiant and flaming energies of the most holy and blessed Trinity.

Notes

[1] See text in Gerasimos Mikragiannanites, *Akolouthia tou hosiou kai theophorou patros hemon kai didaskalou Nikodemou tou Hagioreitou,* ed. Geron Ananias of the Skourtaion monastery, 2nd ed. (1965), pp. 3-4.

[2] Ibid.

[3] C. Cavarnos, *Anchored in God* (Athens, 1959), p. 210.

[4] "He eis hosion anakeryxis Nikodemou tou Hagioreitou," *Ekklesia,* 32 (1955) 137-38.

[5] "Ho hagios Nikodemos kai ta Orthodoxa Aitemata," *Ekklesia,* 33 (1956) 258-59.

[6] *Dictionnaire de Théologie catholique,* 11, 486-90. *Kivotos* (1955), 64-65.

[7] Theokletos Dionysiates, *Hagios Nikodemos ho Hagioreites* (Athens, 1959).

[8] Constantine Cavarnos, *St. Nicodemos the Hagiorite* (Belmont, Mass., 1974), pp. 96-144. Not only has Dr. Cavarnos translated the "Life" of Saint Nikodemos in English (written originally in Greek by the great Hagiorite monk, Gerasimos Mikragiannanites), but he has also translated selected passages from the works of Saint Nikodemos and has presented to us an almost complete list of Saint Nikodemos' works.

[9] Ibid. pp. 66-67.

[10] Dionysiates, *Hagios Nikodemos,* p. 30.

[11]Ibid. pp. 30-31.

[12]Constantine Cavarnos, *Saint Macarios of Corinth*, (Belmont, Mass. 1972).

[13]See the work of Nikodemos' friend for almost thirty-five years; Euthymios, "Vios kai politeia kai agones tou hosiologiotatou kai makaritou kai aoidimou Nikodemou Monachou," *Gregorios Palamas* 4, (1920), 636-41, 5, (1921), 210-18 and Onouphrios Ivirites, "Vios en synopsei tou makaritou kai aoidimou didaskalou Nikodemou Hagioreitou, in Nikodemos' *Paulou hai Dekatessares Epistolai* (Venice, 1819).

[14]Dionysiates, *Hagios Nikodemos*, p. 90.

[15]Mikragiannanites, "Akolouthia" in Cavarnos, *St. Nikodemos*, pp. 79-80.

[16]Cavarnos, *St. Nikodemos*, pp. 79-80 and 93.

[17]Ibid. p. 94.

[18]*Chrestoetheia ton Christianon*, (4th ed., Volos, 1957), p. 320; Cavarnos, *St. Nikodemos*, p. 127.

[19]*Chrestoetheia*, p. 326; Cavarnos, *St. Nicodemos*, p. 128.

[20]Dionysiates, p. 274.

[21]*Gymnasmata Pneumatika* (Thessalonike, 1971), p. 206; Cavarnos, *St. Nicodemos*, p. 123.

[22]*Symvouleutikon Encheiridion* (2nd ed., Athens, 1885), p. 155; Cavarnos, *St. Nicodemos*, pp. 123-34.

[23]*Paulou hai Dekatessares Epistolai*, p. 22; Cavarnos, *St. Nicodemos* p. 124.

[24]Dionysiates, *Ekklesia* 33 (1956), 258.

[25]*Symvouleutikon*, p. 158; Cavarnos, *Saint Nicodemos*, p. 125.

[26]*Gymnasmata*, p. 204.

[27]*Viblos psychophelestate ton en hagiois pateron hemon Varsanouphiou kai Ioannou* (Volos, 1960), p. 83.

[28]Constantine Cavarnos, *St. Macarios of Corinth* (Belmont, Mass., 1972).

[29]A list of the writers in Nikodemos' *Philokalia* is found in *Early Fathers from the Philokalia*, trans. E. Kadloubovsky and G.E.H. Palmer (London, 1969), pp. 416-17.

[30]*Early Fathers from the Philokalia* p. 414.

[31]*Evergetinos* (Athens, 1957-1966). This edition was published in four volumes.

[32]Dionysiates, *Hagios Nikodemos*, pp. 208-12, 219-23.

[33]*Unseen Warfare*, trans. E. Kadloubovsky and G.E.H. Palmer with an introduction by H.A. Hodges (London 1949).

[34]*The Rudder* (Chicago, 1957), p. x.

[35]Ibid.

[36]*Gymnasmata*, p. 211ff.

[37]Ibid. p. 445.

[38]Ibid. p. 312.

[39]*Neon Martyrologion* (Athens, 1961), p. 24.

[40]Dionysiates, *Hagios Nikodemos*, pp. 108-16, 203-08.

[41]*Vivlion psychophelestaton peri tes synechous metalepseos ton achranton tou*

Christou mysterion (Volos, 1961), pp. 60ff.

[42]Ibid. pp. 62ff.

[43]Steven Runciman, *The Great Church in Captivity* (Cambridge, 1968), p. 158.

[44]*Heortodromion* (Venice 1836) pp. 17-18.

[45]*Chrestoetheia*, p.18; Cavarnos, *St. Nicodemos*, p. 126.

[46]*Symvouleutikon*, p. 196; Cavarnos, *St. Nicodemos*, p. 136.

[47]Theokletos Dionysiates, *Athonika Anthe* (Athens, 1962), pp. 294-96.

[48]Kosta M. Mantzouranes, *Nikodemos ho Hagioreites kai ethnapostole* (Naxos, 1963).

[49]Mantzouranes, *Nikodemos*, pp. 35-37.

[50]*Neon Martyrologion* (Athens, 1961), pp. 13, 14, 15, 44, 67ff.

[51]For the Kollyvades movement, see the recent studies by Charilaos S. Tzogas, *He peri mnemosynon eris en Hagio Orei kata ton IH aiona* (Thessalonike, 1969) and Konstantinos K. Papoulides, *To kinema ton Kollyvadon* (Athens, 1971). See also reviews of these studies by Nomikos M. Vaporis in *The Greek Orthodox Theological Review*, 19 (1974) 203-08.

[52]*Unseen Warfare*, p. 77 and Cavarnos, *St. Nikodemos*, p. 131.

[53]*Nea Klimax* (Volos, 1956), p. 247; Cavarnos, *St. Nicodemos*, pp. 138-39.

[54]*Epitome ek ton prophetanaktodautikon psalmon* (Athens, 1864); Cavarnos, *St. Nicodemos*, p. 139.

[55]*Aoratos Polemos* (Athens, 1957), pp. 166ff; Cavarnos, *St. Nicodemos*, p. 141.

[56]*Aoratos Polemos* (Athens, 1957), p. 166; Cavarnos, *St. Nicodemos*, pp. 141-42.

[57]*Symvouleutikon Encheiridion* (Athens, 1885), pp. 116-17; Cavarnos, *St. Nicodemos*, p. 142.

[58]*Symvouleutikon Encheiridion*, pp. 117-21; Cavarnos, *St. Nicodemos*, pp. 143-45.

[59]*Nea Klimax* (Volos, 1956), p. 112; Cavarnos, *St. Nicodemos*, p. 145.

[60]Ibid.

[61]*Pedalion* (Athens, 1957), pp. 53-54, 56-57, 312-313; *The Rudder* (Chicago, 1957), pp. 68-76.

[62]*Christoetheia* (Volos, 1957), pp. 27, 41, 75, 194.

[63]Ibid. pp. 292ff.

[64]Ibid. pp. 144ff.

[65]*Paulou hai Dekatessares Epistolai Hermeneuthesai* 2, 147.

[66]*Aoratos Polemos* (Athens, 1967), p. 160; *Unseen Warfare*, p. 199.

[67]*Aoratos Polemos*, p. 159; *Unseen Warfare*, p. 198. For a more recent discussion, see: *Nicodemos of the Holy Mountain: A Handbook of Spiritual Counsel* (trans. Peter Chamberas); Introduction by George S. Bebis; Preface by Stanley S. Harakas (New York, 1989), p. 24ff.